DATE DUE

JUL 2 7 1983			
AUG 1 0 1983			
GAYLORD			PRINTED IN U.S A

POWER AND MORALITY

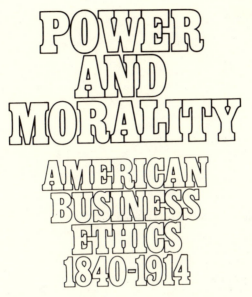

POWER AND MORALITY

AMERICAN BUSINESS ETHICS 1840-1914

Saul Engelbourg

CONTRIBUTIONS IN ECONOMICS
AND ECONOMIC HISTORY,
NUMBER 28

GREENWOOD PRESS

Westport, Connecticut ● London, England

Library of Congress Cataloging in Publication Data

Engelbourg, Saul, 1927–
  Power and morality.

  (Contributions in economics and economic
history ; no. 28 ISSN 0084-9235)
  Bibliography: p.
  Includes index.
  1. Business enterprises—United States—Moral
and religious aspects—History. 2 Business
ethics. I. Title.
HF5343.E54   174′ .4′0973   79-8288
ISBN 0-313-20871-9

Library of Congress Catalog Card Number: 79-8288
ISBN: 0-313-20871-9
ISSN: 0084-9235

First published in 1980

Greenwood Press
A division of Congressional Information Service, Inc.
88 Post Road West, Westport, Connecticut 06881

Printed in the United States of America
10 9 8 7 6 5 4 3 2 1

To the memory of my parents

CONTENTS

FOREWORD

Saul Engelbourg's theme is the evolutionary nature of the thorny subject of business ethics: its rapidly changing nature during the few short decades in which modern business society developed; the efforts of businessmen to solve by themselves the dilemma of ethical behavior in a society that was suspicious of material gain yet deeply appreciative of acquisitive ability; and the increasing transference of these concerns to government and other social agencies. His balanced synthesis of a very large and heterogeneous literature, which he has mastered thoroughly, has resulted in a book on a subject that no one who makes or carries out policy in government or business, or teaches others to do so, can afford to ignore. It will be read and used widely in the coming years when the subject of business and society is one of our most pressing national concerns.

ALBRO MARTIN
Harvard University
Graduate School of
Business Administration

PREFACE

"The ways to enrich are many, and most of them are foul." Francis Bacon's bitter accusation was uttered centuries earlier, yet it typifies criticisms of a later era of economic growth known in its own time and since as the age of the robber barons. The implication is that such colossi as Vanderbilt, Gould, and Rockefeller, as well as lesser figures, could not have risen so high by fair means only and that those who failed did so because they would not or could not resort to fraud. Business behavior of 1880 would have been largely immoral in 1780 and would be largely immoral by 1980. But was this supposition true? Was the morality of big businessmen in fact different in 1914 from what it was about 1840? Was the change, if any, unilinear, or were there fluctuations? How can one account for whatever pattern or patterns existed?

This book is a study of trends in the behavior of big businessmen from 1840 to 1914, and more especially their changing perceptions of that behavior. Its focus is less on practice than on aspiration and rationale; it synthesizes and interprets diverse materials. Its purpose is to present a history of morals but not to moralize.

*   *   *   *

Because business morality is a nebulous term, I have selected certain clearly definable practices for detailed examination. My selection, in addition to prevalence, reflects two principal criteria: conflict between the standards of the particular business element involved and those of business in general, and conflict between the standards of business in general and those of society as a whole. Since my approach is sociological rather than philo-sophical, my stress is on the views of contemporaries. If they considered a practice unethical, I accord this opinion great weight. The views of posterity are valuable chiefly in providing a sense of perspective, a measurement of change.

The specific issues I consider are: conflict of interest, restraint of trade, competitive tactics, stock watering, and financial re-porting. Each of these posed novel challenges to businessmen, and their ultimate resolution was not the same in 1914 as it had been seventy-five years earlier.

* * * *

The lowest rank of business behavior is that in which the businessman disobeys the law (which expresses the minimum standard of morality) whenever it seems expedient and relatively safe to do so. He may seek to justify himself by denying that the law is right.

The next higher rung of business behavior is that in which businessmen disobey the law, often furtively, sometimes openly, as part of commonly accepted behavior in their industry or in all industries. In these circumstances, the individual conforms to his peer group and in this manner justifies himself. The rational-ization is that if enough people commit an act, then it is right even if it is not legal.

The middle position is occupied by those who grudgingly obey the law. One may, however, obey the law and still not be moral.

Above that level is the position of those who obey the law and additionally adhere to a still higher ethical standard in accord with a currently prevailing ideal.

The highest-ranking and most moral businessmen are those who not only obey the law but also initiate a pattern of behavior that is more rigorous and elaborate than that required by either the law or the existing moral code. Innovation is especially important if it applies to an acknowledged leader, since the moral-ity is then socially as well as individually creative.

* * * *

The history of business morals cannot be as easily divided into periods as political history can. Furthermore, the three-quarters of a century under scrutiny does not exhibit distinct turning points. Hence the periodization I have employed is even more than usually arbitrary. The point of departure, circa 1840, approximates the beginning of the economy's transformation to an industrial society; the terminal point, 1914, is intended to indicate its completion. For the first subperiod, 1840–1880, marked by the emergence of large-scale enterprise and the interaction of railroads and industry, the Hepburn investigation of 1879 yields information on business ethics. The Industrial Commission of 1900–1902 sheds light on the period 1880–1900, continuing the theme of evolving moral standards among managers of large-scale enterprise, but with the added factor of two landmarks of federal legislation: the Interstate Commerce Act of 1887 and the Sherman Antitrust Act of 1890. Treatment of the final subperiod, 1900–1914, emphasizes the world of high finance and utilizes both the Armstrong insurance investigation of 1906 and the Pujo money trust investigation of 1912. Also, during the early twentieth century the modern regulatory state began to take shape. By the end of this epoch of seventy-five years, not only the American economy but also the business morality of its managing directors had perceptibly and irrevocably changed.

ACKNOWLEDGMENTS

Ralph W. Hidy is the progenitor of this topic. During my year as Business History Fellow at the Harvard Business School, 1961–1962, he discussed it with me at length and guided the research and the first draft. Thereafter, his interest in this study, and in my career more generally, never flagged. Even as late as February 1977, not long before his death, when I had virtually lost faith, he continued to encourage me. At an intermediate stage, others read succeeding drafts and helped me find my way: Alfred D. Chandler, Jr., Thomas C. Cochran, Eugene Genovese, Julia Weissman, Robert Sobel, and an unnamed publisher's reader. Finally, after Greenwood Press had accepted my manuscript for publication, Robert V. Bruce and Albro Martin read the penultimate draft. Each of these individuals contributed ideas and information and, more vital than either, a sense of direction and style. Lest others think me churlish, my wife, Charlotte Frances, not only read every word more times than either she or I would like to recall, but she also suffered with me and with my work all these years. Every scholar must bear the ultimate responsibility for his work. For better or worse, this work is mine, and such deficiencies as still exist no doubt remain because of my inability to profit from all of the excellent advice tendered.

A historian would be remiss if he failed to accord due recognition to those who serve the cause of scholarship: the librarians and their libraries. The great bulk of the research was conducted at Baker Library of the Harvard Business School. I also consulted materials at the Boston Public Library and Mugar Library of Boston University.

To all of these, and to their fellows elsewhere, I say thanks.

POWER AND MORALITY

I

THE PROCESS OF CHANGE

In a complex and dynamic society, specific situations arise that are not clearly embraced in the existing ethical code, leaving the individual to determine the morality of his own behavior. A moral code evolved by an agricultural, small-scale, personal society, like that of the United States until about 1840, is not wholly applicable to a commercial, large-scale, impersonal society. Furthermore, the new conditions give rise to conflicts between different elements in the existing code, again forcing the individual to make his own choice, without adequate and consistent guidelines.

In the earlier, simpler, and perhaps mythical epoch in the new republic, the opportunities for transgression from the accustomed rules of business behavior were limited in number and geographic scope, the rules were well established, violations were easily perceived and penalized, and in general a harmony was felt to exist between the self-interest of the individual and the interest of the community. But in the United States during the period from 1840 to 1914, many segments of society, particularly businessmen, promoted dynamic change. A national economy replaced a localized one, the size of the representative firm increased, and the nature of competition altered. The economy that was characteristic of 1840 was virtually completely transformed by 1914.

One of the outcomes of this vast change was that some men schooled in one age lived to dominate another. Many of them thus carried the ethos of the old school and were not aware that some of their practices were no longer considered ethical. The new code had not yet stabilized sufficiently to provide them with a fixed reference point. In a world of decentralized decision making, each businessman had to define his own moral standards. His self-interest was still presumed to be congruent with the community interest. But if in the new era the businessman operated on that presumption, he would certainly act in ways that others, then or later, would call into question on moral grounds.

*   *   *   *

Some of the changes in the business ethic came from within the business community, some from without. The internal impetus for redefining honesty originated in the great range of conditions, interests, and behavior. For example, investors in the Northeast, a capital-surplus region, shared moral concerns regarding financial reporting and conflict of interest that were not felt in the West, a capital-deficit section. And the former, hesitantly and haltingly, imposed its standards on the latter. Perhaps this example accounts for the morality of John Murray Forbes of Boston (a leading capital market) in the management of the Chicago, Burlington & Quincy during the revolution of 1875 in which Forbes and his allies ejected from the management those insiders who had violated the implicit conflict-of-interest rules. Some businessmen like Forbes on their own initiative adopted a business morality that preceded governmental concern and later became the model for subsequent action by government. The mere existence of such a moral exemplar helped change business morality.

Another source of the change may have been fostered by growth itself. For example, did the canal and railroad, in developing a national market, increase the extent of competition and thereby alter its very nature? The difficulty in improving business morality from within is the fear, often justified, that competitors will not adopt the same new standards. Thus the stress of the competitive situation tends to put a strain on morality, and the peer group more readily changes for the worse rather than for the better. This hypothesis surely helps to account for the behavior of the participants in railroad pools and railroad wars, as well as the difficulty of eliminating railroad discrimination through voluntary action.

An internal impetus for change also worked through outside agencies such as the government. A businessman may attack a seemingly iniquitous practice of another business group partly out of self-interest and partly out of a concern for the commonweal. The opposition to rebating and other forms of discrimination by the railroads, for example, was led by shippers who believed that they were the victims rather than the beneficiaries of the established system. Such businessmen participated in molding the public conscience and thereby in determining the legislative policy of the state. Francis B. Thurber, Simon Sterne, and other self-styled spokesmen for New York shippers stimulated a groundswell of public concern that eventuated in railroad regulation. The evolving public conscience expressed a new and extensive awareness of a particular moral issue. The press, both popular and business, played a key role here and served as a deterrent to immoral behavior.

With the rapid economic change occuring in the 1800s, the individual was left to define the rules for himself. The traditional business morality gave way slowly and at an uneven rate in connection with different practices and different industries.

Finally cumulative abuses revealed the need for a new morality.[1] Nevertheless, only gradually did society assert its power to define morality and thereby bring the abuses under control. Government thus acted both as a theoretically impartial policeman and as a bodyguard highly partial in practice to whomever exerted the greatest influence. For instance, at the turn of the twentieth century the four dominant meat packers pushed for stringent sanitary regulation of their industry, knowing that their smaller marginal competitors could not afford the cost of higher standards of sanitation.

Restructuring the economy required redesigning business procedures in order to restrain business behavior. "Large scale manipulation of the social order," wrote Aldous Huxley, "can do much to preserve individuals from temptations which, before the reforms, were ever-present and almost irresistible."[2] Separating the corporate stock register from the stock transfer agent ruled out certain types of stock fraud, for example. Accordingly, this kind of transformation had a profound influence on business ethics. Society not only removed temptation by revising the way in which business was conducted but also deterred unethical behavior by penalizing those who could not resist such temptation as remained.

Ultimately, the conditions that precipitated the process of revision were brought under control. For example, railroad rebates, a burning issue until the early twentieth century, ceased as a result of the internalization of a new morality by both railroads and shippers, of the combination of the railroads into a few large systems, and of effective government regulation. The change by no means ended unethical behavior by businessmen, but at least rules had been adopted that enabled society to cope with the problem routinely. Morality caught up with social change, and as long as social change did not accelerate too rapidly, the rules sufficed for a time.

Since the period of revolutionary economic change began, American society in general and American businessmen in particular have been struggling to adapt a code of ethics. When face-to-face transactions were replaced by transactions among dispersed individuals, did the possibility and likelihood of moral transgression increase? A modern critic of entrepreneurial behavior during the Jacksonian era moralized: "As the private conscience grew increasingly powerless to impose restraints on the methods of business, the public conscience, in the form of the democratic government, had to step in to prevent the business community from tearing the society apart in its pursuit of profit."[3] The traditional constraints of the old way were supplemented by the new government.

Individuals insist on higher and more rigorous standards of ethical behavior toward members of their own group than toward outsiders. As America became commercialized in the course of the nineteenth century it shifted from tribal brotherhood to universal otherhood, with one standard applicable to insiders, such as directors, and another to outsiders, such as stockholders. Ethics in dealings between those within a trade or occupation were higher than in dealings with customers or clients. But if the ethical standard within a group is not high enough, then the group loses its cohesiveness, and its internal business cannot be conducted at all, or only with great difficulty.

Those who associate closely are frequently, if not continuously, engaged in transactions in which implicit trust must be close to absolute. Property may be sold at auction with no more than a nod of a head, and a stock or commodity exchange also relies on the most casual sort of agreement to constitute a morally as well as legally binding contract. Credit is based in part on character, because it requires that the lender be able to accept the financial reports of the borrower regarding collateral (such as inventory, warehouse receipts, or accounts receivable) that the lender cannot verify except at considerable expense. The misrepresentation of collateral for a loan places a businessman beyond the pale of other businessmen.

Such internal honesty is essential to the functioning of business. This is the difference between the particularistic and universalistic ethic. During the period under study, this was a prime shift in the business code. The universalistic ethic protects all people within a society. The age-old universalistic rule was *caveat emptor*. The particularistic ethic shields a specific category of people but need not apply even to a closely related category. Businessmen readily and justifiably applied a different code to themselves from that applied to the rest of society. Similarly, one group of businessmen may have a different code from that of another.

Much of the dishonesty in American business was encouraged by the existence of many large-scale, widely owned corporate enterprises with varying values, each competing for the loyalty of the individual. A form of organization similar to feudalism thus ensued in which the enterprise resembled the lord as the center of power. The individual frequently became loyal to the enterprise that provided his sustenance, just as in an earlier era he had been loyal to the lord. In neither case was such an individual loyal to all of the values of the total society.

The morality of the individual is also influenced by the special group that commands his loyalty. The concept of treason bears this out. In one classic example of an agonizing moral decision, Robert E. Lee cast his lot with Virginia and the Confederacy and thus committed treason to the Union. Had he acted in the reverse

way, it might be contended, and it surely would have been contended by some Virginians at the time, that he had committed
treason against Virginia. Businessmen during this period were
confronted with a conflict of loyalties and values, and they had to
make not a single choice but rather a never-ending sequence of
choices concerning their business behavior.

Many businessmen made the goals of their firm the ultimate
values, and the firm was able to command the all but ultimate
loyalty of businessmen, for a variety of reasons. At the time
numerous sources of values, which themselves were amorphous,
were contesting for adherents. In all probability not fully cognizant of the conflict, many businessmen tried to subsume the
conflicting values into one array that seemed defensible, and they
had to rank the values, often unaware that they were doing so.
Consequently, many businessmen performed acts on behalf of the
enterprise that were comparable to acts performed on behalf of
the state, although the implications of this were not perceived. An
example would be the misrepresenting of facts to a supplier,
customer, competitor, or government official. None of these acts
was judged by society as having been performed by individuals
for their own direct benefit.

It seems likely that the idea of the soulless corporation arose at
this time. Businessmen, as agents of change for the corporation,
thus found it possible to act in ways they could not act as individuals, because they did not feel personally responsible. One
railroad executive is supposed to have observed insightfully; "I
have done many things as president that I would not do as a man."[4]

Outrageous behavior, however, forces others to react, and this
is what happened in late nineteenth-century America. When
large, powerful enterprises developed, their managers could and
did do the same things that small abusinessmen did, but individual
and group complaints arose and tended to bring government
action. Of course, every businessman in a small town watched his
competitor's prices, customers, and sources of supply; but when
Standard Oil— which had a power no small-scale enterprise
could equal—kept track of its competitors, opponents called the
practice spying. Large-scale enterprises began to be condemned
for behavior that had not been challenged previously, and with

justice, because now more people were hurt and often more severely.

In the face of a conflict in moral values, ultimately businessmen must accept and adjust to some of the views of the community if they are to avoid public censure. Ethical self-regulation demands the internalization of some of the moral values of the community if freedom from public regulation is to be continued and if up-grading in business ethics is to take place.

*   *   *   *

Business is such a keystone of American society that it is some-what surprising that so little has been written on the history of American business ethics. Possibly there is an implicit belief that business morality has never changed. Nevertheless certain practices that were once quite common—for example, railroad freight rate discrimination—are not today. And the attitude of businessmen toward these practices is different. The fact is that ethics have changed. The reason is that businessmen were categorically different from Americans in general and not simply slightly specialized, sometimes more successful versions of what many others aspired to be and counted on becoming. Perhaps business-men, in their pursuit of self-interest, pressed on the limits of business morality and strained them for a time until a reversal set in as a consequence of both internal and external reactions. It has been alleged that the behavior of businessmen was worse than that of the community at large. This was the impression of so knowledgeable an observer as Arthur H. Cole, a leading analyst of business history: "Business has had a disproportionate share of actors who, even by the standards of their times and discounting the occasions when they were merely outwitting one another, must be set down as performing society a disservice, if not behaving as outright rascals."[5] This opinion may be correct, but it must be regarded as not proven.

The rules of business behavior of the early nineteenth century were appropriate to that world. They defined in a workable fashion the proper conduct of the individual, and the individual responded in a traditional manner. "Thou shalt not steal" was a comprehensible and practicable guide to action because the word *steal* had only a limited number of recognized meanings that could be applied readily to all circumstances.

When enterprises were all small and of approximately equal power, some succeeded and some failed because of differentials in managerial talent, location, luck, and innumerable other variables. But large-scale enterprises triumphed at least in part because of economies of scale. Typically contemporaries, especially those who failed, did not recognize this reason. The losers protested time and again that they could produce as cheaply as anyone else. The logical inference was that others won over them by an unfair advantage.

Following these protests by customers, competitors, and the public at large, change was slow in coming. Individual business-men first had to become aware of the special advantages accruing to some of their competitors, and their protests were often frustrated by the disbelief of others and by their doubts that the accusations, even if true, were a matter of moral concern. Sometimes business-men who were suffering discovered that only those located in a particular region were afflicted. Often they found it an arduous task to publicize their tales of woe because newspapers and period-icals were frequently not interested. And they may have had difficulty in obtaining facts that could be legally proved. For this reason, businessmen again and again relied on associations of one sort or another to arouse the public and to augment their strength. Finally, interest groups called upon government to right the wrong. Legislative hearings, as in the case of the Hepburn in-vestigation of 1879, were utilized to collect information, gain command of the front page, and finally prepare the groundwork for legislation such as the Interstate Commerce Act and the Sherman Antitrust Act.

The next step by the beleaguered businessmen was to publicize their cause, making individuals cognizant of the significance of their own actions and mobilizing public opinion. More and more spokesmen joined the clamor. There was now a market for news-papers and periodicals prepared to denounce business practices considered unethical. Legislative campaigns were organized, and finally acts were passed defining the "immorality."

As time passed these new rules became the rules by which businessmen worked. Means became more important relative to ends. Even the successful, or those who aspired to be successful, abandoned practices that had once been quite routine. The new came to be virtuous as the old had been, although the virtues were not identical. The goal remained the same—the great achievement —but the way was now straighter and narrower.

2 THE EMERGENCE OF POWER AND RESTRAINT 1840~1880

Between 1840 and 1880, businessmen in the United States expanded the size of the representative firm and created some unusually large-scale enterprises, notably in transportation and communication. It was during these years that companies such as the New York Central and Pennsylvania railroads attained their dominance. In these industries and a few others, concentration of control in the hands of a few was marked by a new pattern of competition, later labeled oligopoly. Practices (both inherited and new) that were in time denounced as immoral became more significant because of these modifications in the scale, range, and organization of businesses.

The leaders of business during this era typically had acquired their sense of business morality in an age of almost rustic simplicity. Before 1840, the distinction between insiders and outsiders was of little consequence, the universalistic ethic dominated with few challenges from the particularistic, and the business morality was widely shared, with few businessmen changing or even thinking about change. In contrast, the years following 1840 witnessed a great upheaval in the economy, an industrial revolution that stemmed in part from a drastic reduction in the cost of transportation and a consequent expansion of the market and a large change in the morality based on that economy. The early close-knit community in which all businessmen knew each other gave way gradually and unevenly to an extensive community composed of strangers. The rate of change in business morality during this era was relatively slow and was, in fact, more or less constant until the mid-seventies. The moral climate was no worse in 1870 than in 1840, but the variety and number of actors was greater, and the leading actors were more powerful. I suggest, therefore, that a change in moral standards was brought about by those who suffered from the new situation; in short, power generated restraint.

CONFLICT OF INTEREST

Conflict of interest was not a problem in small-scale enterprises in the early nineteenth century. Most of these were sole proprietorships so, of course, the manager could not cheat the owner; they were the same person. (Such opportunities did exist in a partnership but only in a very limited way.) But when the size of enterprises began to grow, and ownership and control became separate, conflict of interest became a more serious issue. Members of the board of directors, representatives of the now more numerous stockholders, and upper-level management employees could and did hold decision-making positions in large-scale corporate enterprises in which they were not significant owners. The practice of inside contracting provides a classic conflict-of-interest situation. By buying from or selling to an enterprise in which they had a large financial interest, these insiders could set terms that would divert excessive profits from the firm they managed to the firm they owned.[1] At first, the crucial distinction between the controllers and the owners of concerns was not clearly comprehended.[2] As it became plainer, and as its potential for unfair gain became evident to more and more victims, such as the minor stockholders, these practices drew increasing fire, and government became interested in the problem.

The organization of business with such potential conflict of interest was common from 1840 to 1880. Yet by 1880, most of these unfair practices had declined in frequency or diminished.

In the year 1870 it was the commonest thing in the world for the president of a large corporation to use his position as as means of enriching himself and his friends at the expense of the stockholders in general;

and it might almost be added it was the rarest thing in the world for
anyone to object. . . . Ten years later things had improved. It was no
longer considered proper for a president to wreck his company in order
to enrich himself. Yet even in this decade . . . the public . . . saw no
harm if he used his inside information to get rich at the expense of any-
body and everybody else.[3]

Throughout this period, many firms were treated as if they were
personal instruments for the use of the managers and his supporters. If he possessed control, the president could disregard all
other interests.

A brazen case involving Robert Schuyler, both the president of
the New Haven Railroad and its stock transfer agent, contributed
to the process of change. In 1854, the curiosity of a fellow director
led to the realization that Schuyler had issued stock that he used for
his personal advantage as collateral on which to borrow. In doing
this he had also falsified the railroad's stock books.[4] Henry Varnum
Poor, a noted business journalist with a concern for the interests of
his readers, recommended, as a means of preventing a recurrence,
the creation of a separate stock register to cross-check the stock
transfer agent, and this procedure was quickly adopted by most railroads.[5] Thus the power of the insider to prey on others in this
fashion was ended.

Such an improved institutional device, as well as the morality
of the individual, serves to alter the behavior of businessmen.
Poor was not an insider. His role as outsider in meliorating the
behavior of the business community was facilitated by the development of a body of investors and of a press that catered to
them. The press, both general and specialized, exposed the questionable activities of businessmen and in so doing aroused readers
and made them concerned. The press also suggested the remedy,
presented it to the decision makers (in this instance, the railroad
management), and thereby contributed to its adoption. Occasionally the press clamored for governmental action, which it eagerly
reported.

One of the situations that hastened the clarification and demise
of conflict of interest featured David A. Neal, who in the 1850s

was a land speculator and at the same time a director of the Illinois Central Railroad with a special responsibility for managing the railroad's lands. William H. Osborn, president of the railroad, thought that Neal's interest in his own land speculations frequently was inconsistent with his responsibilities to the company. Osborn conjectured that such land-speculating directors would transfer to their own account much of the profit that belonged to the railroad. For this reason and others, Neal was removed from his control of the railroad's Land Department.[6] What on the surface appeared to be a dispute over the profits derived from land altered the moral behavior of the individual. The conflict of interest was resolved by removing the individual from a position in which the conflict was possible; the insider was thereafter precluded from using his position for his own self-interest to the detriment of the interests of others.

Conflict of interest also potentially existed because of services that businesses required. Railroad construction provides a prime example. Some railroads served as their own prime contractors and subcontracted individual parts of the work to outside firms not otherwise connected with the railroad, and others employed outside firms to bear the responsibility for the entire work. The railroads wanted a large amount of work accomplished in a short time, and specialized construction firms had the requisite skill, experience, and equipment.

The conflict of interest arose when railroad insiders organized a special construction company to construct the railroad they headed. These insiders thus acted as both buyers and sellers. On this point, both nonparticipating insiders and outsiders offered criticism. Henry Varnum Poor in the 1850s objected to the "contracting directors," because such men would have few qualms about profiting at the expense of the ordinary stockholders and bondholders.[7] In 1857 John Murray Forbes, an insider in the Chicago, Burlington & Quincy Railroad, condemned railroads that permitted this practice, charging in a letter that "some railroads have been built by *contractors*, who were directors, and pronounced upon the proper execution of their own work." His own railroad, in contrast, was "run by honest and very intelligent men, simply and purely for the interest of the stockholders, and not for any . . . individual."[8]

But stockholders frequently lamented that their interests were not properly represented by the managers of the enterprise. George D. Phelps, president of the Delaware, Lackawanna & Western, complained in the late 1850s that some directors, such as Moses Taylor, a merchant as well as a coal and iron entrepreneur, were favoring their own interests at the expense of the railroad. Phelps called for improved business morality and lessened conflict of interest. Instead he was forced to resign, and the stockholders' meeting upheld the directors, as did an investigating committee.[9] The protest of the president, although not sustained by the owners of a majority of the shares, did attract the attention of a larger audience, minimally the stockholders but others as well, to the participation of the directors in a conflict-of-interest situation.

Another version of conflict of interest manifested itself when Daniel Drew resigned as treasurer of the Erie Railroad in 1857 on the complaint of other stockholders that he owned stock in steamships and railroads that connected with the Erie. Drew acknowledged that others viewed his outside activities as inconsistent with his position in the Erie, thus implicitly conceding the existence of a moral issue.[10] There is little, if any, indication that this occurrence affected Drew's subsequent notorious career as a manipulator of the Erie.

Railroads were enormous purchasers of everything from nuts and bolts to rails and rolling stock, creating numerous opportunities for insiders to take advantage of. Erastus Corning, a merchant and iron manufacturer as well as a railroad president, was one of the pioneers in the practice of making favorable contracts with himself to sell supplies to his railroads.[11] Corning was president of the New York Central Railroad and served in that capacity without salary.[12] The relationship between Corning and the New York Central resulted in an inquiry in 1855 by a stockholders' committee. Despite the fact that the committee was composed of his friends, its report was critical of Corning and recommended against the railroad's buying from stockholders.[13] However, the Central continued to buy from Corning. In 1863 the *New York Tribune* balked: "Paying him by allowing him to furnish the road with every spike, chair, bolt, butt, screw, etc., it may need, out of his own store, at his own price, will never do. Ten per cent per annum can never be got [by the railroad stockholders] that way." The *Tribune* demanded that Corning either work literally for nothing or be paid a salary; either alternative would end the conflict of interest.[14] The newspaper, speaking on behalf of the other stockholders, invoked the universalistic ethic that all be treated alike. The call for change was also internal. The self-interest of certain insiders—a committee of stockholders—coincided with principle, raising the standard of business morality.

Two decades later the New York Central, substantially owned by the Vanderbilts, presented quite a different picture. At the Hepburn investigation of 1879, undertaken by a committee of the New York Assembly and instigated by merchants and other shippers who agitated against discriminatory railroad rates, Edwin D. Worcester, the secretary of the Central, testified that "there is nobody that I know of connected with the New York Central Railroad Company that has now or ever did have any interest in any contract for work done on the road." Chauncey M. Depew, the Central's counsel, in his masterful summation before the Hepburn committee, denied that inside companies existed, and, pointedly, William H. Vanderbilt sold his Standard Oil trust certificates when that company became a Central customer.[15]

For purely practical reasons the New York Central Railroad was quite different from other railroads. The Vanderbilts, Cornelius and his son, William H., owned well over half of the stock of the system. They used the Central as though it belonged only to them and had no use for inside operations. The small stockholders did not suffer, because the Vanderbilts did not work in contravention to the interests of their stockholders; to have done so would have been of no benefit to their own holdings. Thus it is readily apparent that conflict of interest thrived not so much because an enterprise was large as because its shares were widely held and separate from management.[16]

In the Burlington, a more conventional railroad with dispersed ownership, some of the directors invested in extensions, the so-called river roads, as feeders to the main line.[17] In return for control, these insiders, led by James F. Joy, president of the Burlington from 1865 to 1871, supplied the necessary cash to the construction company that built the river roads and thereby acted to lower the expected implicit standard of dealing at arm's distance within the Burlington. Intermingling involvements of the Burlington and the river roads are evident not only in the appearance of some men on the boards of both but also in the marketing of river roads bonds by the Burlington (in exchange for a traffic agreement) and the purchase of river roads bonds largely by Burlington investors, relying on the endorsement of the Burlington's directors. The river roads were unable to meet their bond interest payments in 1873, and the Burlington directors decided to use Burlington money for this purpose. John Murray Forbes, the dominant figure in the Burlington, protested to an associate: "I can guess at many good reasons for paying out a large sum to outsiders, but I am utterly at a loss for reasons justifying paying it to ourselves."[18]

The deepening of the crisis brought about by the panic of 1873, one of the major depressions in American history, prevented further financing to complete the river roads. Interest on the bonds could not be met, and the river roads defaulted. This crisis forced an examination by Forbes. Writing to a fellow director of the Burlington, he castigated railroad executives "who represent at least two other companies, whose interests may be conflicting.[19] On a personal inspection trip of the river roads, as Forbes probed more deeply, he became aghast at the effrontery of a man who, as president of the railroad company, paid himself also as president of the construction company. "What the equities or the elements of expediency are, I know not," he pondered, nonplussed.[20]

After Joy, the ringleader of the insiders, denied his responsibility to those Burlington investors who had bought river roads bonds, Forbes damned Joy, telling him:

I then found to my *utter* surprise that you and all the other active directors upon whose judgment I had relied were interested in contracts for the building of the roads . . . that you were practically sellers of the bonds to us outside the ring, and that they and all the assets of the company had belonged to you as contractors—on such terms that with ordinary care (in *my* judgment) you ought to have made among you over a million of dollars by the bargain.[21]

It was this situation that precipitated the revolution of 1875. Forbes fought a proxy battle and forced Joy and others off the Burlington board, an action indicating a change in the code for business executives and justifying the designation "revolution of 1875."[22] Forbes's concept of trusteeship was that of "trustees for others," a phrase he used in a letter to a business ally in 1873, before the storm broke.[23] The others were in part those in the Boston capital market who had bought stock in the Burlington, relying on the high morality and reputation for integrity of its management.

Those who were ejected from the board fought back, insisting that they had done right as they saw it. The points of view diverged, because Forbes stood on a principle while the others resolved the conflict of interest between owners and managers in a pragmatic way by pointing to the result, which had increased the strength of the Burlington.[24] Significantly, public opinion, as manifested by the rallying of the stockholders around Forbes, was beginning to turn against those who were involved in acts for their own benefit rather than for the benefit of the company that employed them. One insider complained: "I am regarded with anxiety by my friends and with doubt by C. B. & Q. stockholders."[25] He had been transformed into a pariah because a segment of the community had imposed sanctions. The outcome of the revolution of 1875 was that "for the Burlington, at least, such dubious practices stood condemned. . . . In the process it had established a new and higher standard of integrity." In 1875 Forbes was responsible for the rule that the president of the Burlington was "to notify every person in the service of the company that to receive any commission or gratuity of any kind . . . upon any negotiation or purchase in its behalf, directly or indirectly, should be followed by immediate expulsion from its service." Thus was the revolution of 1875 broadened into more than a palace revolution. Richard Overton, historian of the Burlington, writes:

As the outcome of the Revolution of 1875 conclusively demonstrated, the men who had so patiently pieced together the Burlington and won for it a secure and respected place among western railroads put a high value on integrity. To their thinking, it was not an idea that one could honor adequately by lip service. It meant dealing honorably within the company, with other railroads, and above all with the community. This, they firmly believed, was the only way to insure success in the long run.[26]

It is difficult to assess the full significance of the revolution of 1875. Regardless of his motives (which may have been mixed), John Murray Forbes chose to stand on high ground and defend a principle. Internally generated, this event affected a major railroad, one of the important capital markets, Boston, and men of both power and repute. It set a new and higher standard (as judged by contemporaries) not only for one railroad but also for enterprises generally, since the Burlington stockholders' meeting was well publicized. Men might, and did, commit acts inimical to the welfare of the enterprises with which they were associated, but no longer could they be blind to the moral status of acts of this character.

Forbes is supposed to have defined his commercial code by advising, "Never [simultaneously] undertake to hunt with the hounds and run with the hares.[27] However, his perceptions were not always the same, as indicated by his comments on Oakes Ames, member of the House of Representatives, a shovel manufacturer, and a railroad promoter. He justified Ames's participation in the Crédit Mobilier, an inside construction company that channeled funds from the Union Pacific, on the basis of the fact that the railroad was actually constructed. Forbes observed:

It was a hard job Oakes Ames had to do in those times and I did not hanker after joining him in the undertaking when he would have given me as good terms as he did his Congressional partners. The Road was much better built—quicker and did work better than such a plan promised or would have been accomplished under any but so strong and energetic a head as Ames. I have always tried to avert blame from him for the mistakes he made.[28]

There is reason to agree with Forbes; the Crédit Mobilier affair was grossly overdrawn by the investigating congressional committee.

Although the inside construction company had been and continued to be for some time to come the characteristic mode of financing railroad construction, the standards regarding inside deals had changed. By the 1870s, condemnation of insiders who benefited personally was being voiced by men who might not have objected earlier. Unanimity of neither behavior nor attitude prevailed throughout the period, but it does appear that the weight of opinion increasingly came on the side of the idea for which Forbes successfully fought. Both before and after the river roads episode, some businessmen expressed themselves in opposition to conflict of interest. William Henry Osborn boasted in 1863 to a former director that "when the history of this corporation [Illinois Central Railroad] is written, it may be safely said that for ten years at least none of its managers used it for private purposes, or profited from it in any way.[29] If nothing else, this self-serving statement indicates an acute awareness of the issue, and at that, a decade before Forbes lashed out at Joy and his associates. Ten years after Osborn's claim, George Washington Cass, Jr., president of the Northern Pacific Railroad, indicated quite plainly that, in order to avoid conflict of interest, he wanted no one associated with a construction company on the directorate of the Northern Pacific.[30] Similarly, Milton H. Smith, an executive of the Louisville & Nashville and later its president, in 1872 addressed a manager of another firm in which he was an investor: "To avoid giving meddlesome people the opportunity of saying that we are using our official positons to foster our individual interests, Mr. [Albert] Fink (who is in my opinion unduly sensitive on this point) wishes to dispose of his interest and desires me to do likewise."[31]

During the Hepburn hearings in 1879, Hugh Jewett, president of the Erie Railroad, was questioned about a contract in which the rolling stock had been purchased from an Erie director. The speed with which he commented on this and similar transactions reveals his perception that this was a serious matter. He interjected, "I recognize . . . that under ordinary circumstances, there ought not to be contracts between a corporation and one of its Directors, beyond the ordinary business contract."[32] By this time the behavior pattern had changed and what had once been commonplace was now infrequent.

Sanctions against insiders operating at the expense of the company were probably first applied to employees and later to directors.[33] "It is indispensable to the preservation of an honest and efficient service from those employed by the Company," as one railroad president put it, "that they should not be engaged in any business which in any way directly or indirectly relates to the Company's business."[34] Similarly, Forbes commented: "I don't question the good faith with which this has been done, but I do think a sixty million corporation can well afford to pay a skillful man for his work, keeping him severely clear of representing any other corporations which have dealings with his main road."[35]

It might be assumed that in general if a man knows what is right, he will do the right, but this is far from invariably the case, particularly in business matters. Joseph W. Suppy, who held numerous middle-management positions with the Erie from 1850 to 1872, was questioned rather sharply during the Hepburn investigation by the Erie counsel about conflict-of-interest incidents during the Jay Gould regime. His answers are of interest not because he himself was a participant and thus profited but because he was caught in the tentacles of the system.

> Q. Why didn't you take some steps, if such a transaction as you have described and as you are finally willing to characterize took place under your nose and you participated in it—why didn't you take steps to make it known?
> A. And I be dismissed?
> Q. I am not asking you about the consequences; why didn't you do it?
> A. I probably never thought of it, because I supposed if I did I would be dismissed.[36]

There was much greater awareness of the moral issue in 1880 than in 1840. As outsiders, the minor stockholders of the affected enterprise objected because they were not gaining, and they exerted heavy pressures; self-interest has a distinct bearing on the morality of the individual. Furthermore, the press and businessmen not directly connected with the particular enterprise privately and publicly reprimanded the insiders.

The individuals involved in a conflict of interest often evinced no concern that they were lowering the standard. They appear to have been blind to the existence of a moral issue, perhaps because such actions were much more widespread at that time and thus appeared to be right. There were also those in the business community, like Forbes and Poor, who did foster a growing moral consciousness and thereby in time effected some improvement in the standard.

RESTRAINT OF TRADE

Morality was an element in the traditional opposition to restraint of trade; and the English common law, representing a distillation of the mores of the community, declared such agreements illegal and unenforceable. Adam Smith, initially a moral philosopher, advocated competition as in the best interests of the community. The structures of the industries in which such restraints evolved in nineteenth-century America had certain similarities: relatively few sellers, high overhead costs with decreasing unit costs as volume increased until an optimum was reached at a high volume, and excess capacity in the industry and in the firms. The combination of these factors was potent. As long as the net covered some fraction of the overhead, each enterprise was induced to reduce prices so as to maximize volume and thereby minimize unit costs. The response to this competitive pressure from the 1840s through the 1870s was commonly either price agreements (loose combinations) or consolidations (close combinations), as well as other collusive practices including the sharing of information and division of markets. In the loose combinations, the independence of the individual firm, and hence its freedom of action, continued; this was indeed its fatal defect. In the close combinations, the independence of the separate enterprises ceased, and control was centralized. Both were but different means to the same ends: stabilizing or increasing prices, production, and profits. Historically, the general public had ambivalent attitudes about restraint of trade, condemning it when the demands of business seemed unreasonable and sanctioning it when necessary to maintain the existing pattern of business.

Transportation agreements, given the conditions of the industry,

developed early and often. A steamboat combination for the
Louisville—New Orleans trade appeared in 1832, and similar
arrangements to sustain prices and regulate markets were used
thereafter throughout the country. The combinations were not
secret, indicating that they were encompassed by the universalistic
ethic, and the agreements were publicized in the local press. They
were generally approved both by the business world and by the
public. This situation was probably related to the concept of the
just price, and eventually regulatory commissions attempted to
set rates at levels that more or less guaranteed the survival of all
but the most inefficient enterprises.

Cornelius Vanderbilt and others were paid by competitors to
keep their boats off the Hudson River.[37] Except for an occasional
newspaper editorial, few objected, perhaps because of the depressed
economic conditions.[38] By 1854, fifteen years later, however,
New York enacted a law against pooling (the allocation of sales or
earnings among competitors in order to fix prices at more than
competitive levels). The passage of the anti-pooling legislation
indicated that the public was no longer so favorably disposed to
price fixing because of changes in the economic circumstances and
an enhanced concern with the power of private enterprise. But the
steamship lines circumvented the law, evidence of immorality.[39]

Pooling was also used on canals. The canal boat companies on
the Pennsylvania Canal for example, organized a pool in 1841. A
year later the transporters were tried and convicted of being a
combination injurious to the public interest.[40] Presumably to
violate a law prohibiting pooling is to violate the moral code of
society, if not that of the business community.

The railroads repeated the behavior of their predecessors, the
steamboats and the canal boats. Officers of the trunk railroads
convened in New York in 1854 and signed an agreement to stabilize
rates and competitive practices for freight and passengers for the
area encompassed by New York City and any points west and
southwest of Buffalo, Pittsburgh, Dunkirk, and Wheeling. *The
New York Times* condemned this agreement as a negation of
competition and hence contrary to the public interest.[41] But a similar group of railroad officials met in 1856 and agreed on freight
and passenger rates. It also tried to cope with the omnipresent

irritation of rate cutting.[42] This last was so annoying that John Murray Forbes found it possible to comment privately, "We can stand a great deal of cheating better than competition."[43]

This was indeed the nub of the problem: businessmen competed and broke a pool by failing to abide by the terms of the agreement, and therefore businessmen could not trust each other under these circumstances. Even now the question of right and wrong is murky (although railroad pooling, under the supervision of the Interstate Commerce Commission, was legalized in 1920). Does the moral businessman sign pooling agreements? Does the moral business-man cheat on his fellow businessmen? Who and what is immoral?

Pooling by railroads, according to its defenders, included such virtues as stability of rates and publication of rates. Pooling also effectively curbed rate discrimination by removing the incentive. Its critics claimed, and some railroad executives agreed, that rates were higher with pooling. A leading railroad critic of the day, Simon Sterne, conceded publicly that the mercantile community found pooling less objectionable than discriminatory rates but opposed the practice because it violated the principle of competition, a keystone of the universalistic ethic, supposedly the protection of the public against excessive rates.[44] Sterne would have come out for pooling (he did later) but feared losing the support of those who backed his pose as a reformer. Ultimately, state and federal regulation brought both maximum and minimum rates under control.

Some railroaders defended pooling on grounds of simple self-interest. Thomas Dickson, president of the Delaware & Hudson Canal Company, believed that combinations to restrict production and maintain prices were proper. "I would be justified by all laws, both human and divine; I would be doing my stockholders an injustice if I didn't."[45]

One railroad expert, Albert Fink, showed a remarkable insight into the nature of pooling and from the outset recognized its monopolistic character and accepted government supervision.[46] Simon Sterne also accepted the desirability of federal regulation but noted that "although they [the railroads] claim that the pooling arrangement answers the public purposes better than what preceded it was instituted because it served the private purposes of the railways better than the chaotic condition that previously existed.[47] In 1886, Sterne told the Cullom committee, a special Senate inquiry into interstate commerce headed by Shelby M. Cullom, that he favored pooling and that he had favored it while counsel to the Hepburn committee.[48] Pooling would provide the railroads with higher profits through higher and more stable rates and the shipper with a halt to discrimination. In short, pooling is an instance in which the interest of the railroads and the shippers, as Sterne implicitly acknowledged, were complementary rather than antagonistic. Public regulation eventually stabilized rates and therefore fulfilled the same function as a pool organized by and for the private interests of the railroads.

Seemingly, something that promised so much to so many ought to have been opposed by none, but in fact pooling agreements were unenforceable as contracts under common law as contrary to the public interest. Pools had no legal standing, were not legally enforceable, and were constantly either being broken or else on the verge of being broken.[49] As new railroads were built, as systems expanded either by construction or consolidation (by the early twentieth century half a dozen or so major systems dominated the American railroad network), or as the control of a system changed hands, the competitive structure underwent stress, with one road trying to expand its share of the business at the expense of those who were satisfied with the *status quo*.

The financial temptation was strong and the enforcement weak. A shipper told the Hepburn committee:

After a pool has been formed I generally make better rates than before; as soon as I see a pool has been formed then I know I can probably do better within a week than before.

Q.   That is to say because railways do not observe their pooling arrangement.
A.   I suppose so.[50]

A contemporary publication observed, "If there is more complaint of broken agreements in railroad business than in most other affairs, it must be remembered that in the railroad business the agreements which are broken are primarily those which the law does not compel us to keep."[51]

Historians are not unanimous as to whether the man who supported a pool or the man who cheated on other members was the more virtuous. So Gilchrist is able to praise Albert Fink for the former, while Grodinsky commends Jay Gould for the latter. Businessmen either joined, adhered to, circumvented, or withdrew from pools apparently as their interests seemed to dictate, all the while accepting pooling as a general principle.

Industry also adopted a number of devices to mitigate the impact of competition and encountered the same instability as a result of cheating. Industrial pooling, common in the antebellum period, flourished when firms were small and unincorporated. The salt pools, for example, engaged in price fixing and output limitation, assigned quotas to member firms, and used joint sales. The combinations were open and well publicized in the press. The participants defended them because of price inelasticity and the right to fair prices. (These arguments, pro and con, are similar to those regarding fair trade.) A prevalent belief in "fairness" deterred public criticism.[52] There were parallel arrangements in cordage and iron, the response of industry to increasing capacity and ruinous competition.[53] Especially after the panic of 1873, in one industry after another there was a seemingly endless cycle of competition, pooling, price cutting, and pooling again.

A means out of the difficulties of the loose combination was close combination through the consolidation of actual or potential competitors and establishment of common ownership by a relatively large number of stockholders. Standard Oil, like many concerns in other industries, pursued a policy of acquiring competitors, although it never achieved an absolute monopoly.[54] This was the first major use of the close combination in industry that led to restraint of trade. Standard Oil Company (Ohio) possessed 10 percent of the industry in the early 1870s and was the largest refiner; a decade later a new Standard Oil combination carried on 85 to 90 percent of the business in the industry.[55] Standard's method of close combination,—it absorbed competitors and thus virtually eliminated domestic competition,—was to prove much more effective than pooling, which contained built-in instability because each enterprise retained its independence. Standard Oil remained an entity until sundered in 1911 as a result of an antitrust suit, while the individual pools came and went. Pooling has long since constituted a *per se* antitrust violation, whereas mergers or close combinations may be legal, and internally generated growth certainly is.

Much of our behavior and values are so much a part of us that we have never examined them critically. So it appears with the businessmen during this era, for an examination of the evidence offers no dialogue on pooling, price agreements, consolidations, or other related efforts of competitors to increase profits. Businessmen had matured in an economy in which such practices long had been completely a matter of course.

Evolution from within was infinitesimal and there was not even any appreciable amount of prodding from without. The power of these combinations was still too new to be comprehended; too few outsiders were as yet adversely affected. The belief in the morality of businessmen coming together for their mutual benefit endured as the dominant value and was implicitly sanctioned by society despite the strictures of the common law. Not until 1890, a decade after the close of the period under consideration, was the common law supplemented by statutory law with the passage of the Sherman Act.

COMPETITIVE TACTICS

The desire to become richer was omnipresent among businessmen and, for that matter, among the populace generally. Competitive tactics were utilized as a means to that end. Although *competitive tactics* is an omnibus term, my focus here is the practice of charging different prices to different buyers for the same commodity or service when this is not justified by cost considerations.

Price discrimination as a means of maintaining an advantage over competitors is as old as antiquity and sanctioned by long usage. It is linked to the tradition of bargaining, which means that a buyer obtains a secret price concession commensurate with his skill in matching wits with the seller. Posted or open prices were not common in the nineteenth century, and even where they did exist, they did not necessarily constitute the final selling price. Initially the contest between buyer and seller was one of skill, and only gradually did it become a test of economic strength as well, when a shipper with bargaining power (a large-volume shipper with alternate ways of shipping his goods) often received freight rates lower than did his competitors.

There is an inextricable relationship between price discrimination and large-scale enterprise, high overhead cost, and competition among the few. Railroads, for example, were large-scale enterprises, with a fixed investment not customarily used to capacity, and there were never more than a few operating between any two points. If each of these few competitors contested actively for business, one way in which a railroad might expand its share of the market was by attracting the customers of others through lower prices. Any rate that exceeded operating cost would defray part of the fixed cost to the railroad's advantage. However, discriminatory pricing was used as a means of having one's cake and eating it; since such a price constituted a concession below the price usually charged, the railroad hoped that it would have to grant reductions to only a few shippers. An open price reduction to all might result in a price war in which no seller would gain. Therefore, both the existence and amount of the discriminatory rate were kept as secret as possible. The technique was to reduce prices secretly and only where competition compelled it and to maintain prices where competition permitted it.

Price discrimination was used early by railroads as a competitive tactic, and equally early it appeared to some as unethical, although not for several decades (owing to inconsistent and divergent values and attitudes concerning railroad freight rate pricing policy) was society sufficiently of one mind to take positive action. Railroad men themselves were troubled by the means that were used to switch customers from one railroad to another. At a railroad conference in 1850, one executive complained:

Means are used to get business from *other roads*, which anyone would be ashamed to resort to in the transaction of private business; which shows that the Managers as well as the Corporation, have *small* souls, if any. We make solemn bargains with each other to be governed by certain principles and rules, and violate them the same day, by a secret bargain with an individual to obtain a small pittance of freight from another road. The people, seeing this, lose all respect for us, and we seem to have none for ourselves; and they approach us to *dicker* with us, like jockies, without even thinking that we might deem it an insult. In this way we have already sunk our characters so low, that the term *"Railroad man"* is one of reproach, and at once destroys his influence in legislative halls, and jeopardizes his rights, and the rights of the corporation even in our courts of justice.[56]

Another delegate a year later also criticized the competitive tactics that railroads used in order to obtain business and claimed that they were not appropriate for honorable men.[57]

During the course of the Hepburn investigation of 1879, the New York railroads, particularly the New York Central and the Erie, probably received the most intensive public scrutiny of any railroads in this era. Discrimination was standard mercantile practice sanctioned by both the business community and society.[58] In the Hepburn hearings a parade of executives from these two major railroads described the scene as they witnessed it from their excellent vantage point. Generally the practices of the Central and the Erie were quite similar, and the evidence is abundant that these two were illustrative of a national phenomenon. Each had discriminatory rates as to products, places, and persons. Indeed special or discriminatory rates were so widespread that the open or scheduled rates were meaningless except as points of departure in bargaining. Rates were set without regard to specific cost. Rather the railroads charged according to their idea of the value of the service, or, as it came to be called, "what the traffic would bear," and altered the rate if it was necessary to prevent the shipper from losing the sale. A related practice was for the railroad to lower the freight classification, which achieved the same end as reducing the rate. In addition, a flat rate was used; it was applied to all classes of freight and was less than the rate for the lowest freight classification. It was common practice to bill at the public rate and rebate the amount above the special rate to the shipper or to the consignee, depending upon the arrangement.[59]

Railroaders considered the shipper morally bound to keep

information about his rates secret. To the extent that this was done, each shipper was precluded from claiming the advantage accorded another, and it may have helped to keep some of them totally ignorant as to the existence of discriminatory rates. In fact, in a Joint Letter submitted to the Hepburn committee, William H. Vanderbilt of the Central and Hugh Jewett of the Erie denied the existence of any discriminatory rates.[60] No credible explanation was offered during the investigation for a statement so contradictory of the later testimony of railroad officials as well as the records of the railroads that were examined. However, one can perhaps account for it by reasoning that the railroads may have believed that their policy of secrecy had been effective. There was apparently a misunderstanding. "Special rate" may mean a rate different from the published rate and available to anyone on demand (Vanderbilt freely acknowledged these); or it may mean a special secret rate available to only one shipper.

Just as railroad men expected to arrange special rates, their customers also expected them. Business leaders of this time had been trained in an era in which prices were set by bargaining and the posted price (if it existed) meant nothing; obtaining a price reduction was a recognized competitive technique and part of the universalistic ethic. The oil industry, on which so much attention has been lavished, began at a time when the one-price concept was in its infancy.[61] The oil refiners simply followed the same tactics as shippers of other products in seeking special treatment from carriers. The typical refiner was a big shipper of a bulky commodity over a long distance, so that the freight rates could well provide a decisive competitive advantage. Secret rate reductions appeared by the mid-1860s and were granted to all large shippers or to those at competitive points.[62] Both the shippers and the carriers kept the net rate secret.[63]

The competitive tactics used in the middle decades of the nineteenth century varied considerably. To a businessman, secrecy was a way of life to a degree scarcely comprehensible to a modern businessman who has learned to live with the Internal Revenue Service, administrative regulatory agencies, and public investigations. The leaders of this epoch learned in their youth, from the customs and mores of the small individualistic enterpriser, to believe in the right of a man to keep secret his operations, which included concessions from suppliers, rebates from railroads, and even the volume of sales or profits.[64] Even legislative inquiries were met with less than the whole truth.

The oil industry was the first to come substantially under the control of a single firm. Standard Oil was the first large-scale manufacturing enterprise with multiple dispersed facilities. Its competitive tactics brought it unwanted notoriety.

During the 1870s Standard Oil grew in absolute size and dominated its industry. It possessed an awesome power which it used to induce competitors to leave the industry. Both Standard Oil and its competitors utilized a clutch of competitive tactics that came to be regarded as morally reprehensible. Standard Oil practiced espionage, but all eagerly sought information as to shipments and sales.[65] It also used local price cutting, and here Standard's staying power gave it an obvious advantage.[66] Individuals who sold out to Standard and did not join it usually signed an agreement prohibiting them from reentering the oil business for a specified period.[67] In employing these and similarly sharp competitive tactics, Standard was in good company since they were an accepted part of the universalistic ethic. Of these, its transportation advantages were of paramount importance to Standard's success.

The railroad network became finer, and competition at some points was keener. Where competition existed, railroads cut rates sharply. This price or rate discrimination was so much a matter of public controversy and legislative investigation that businessmen voiced their opinions freely. An investigation conducted by the state of Pennsylvania in 1867 made public the semisecret discriminatory rate to large shippers and the wholly secret rate to specially favored shippers.[68] The report of the legislative committee condemned discrimination and concluded that as common carriers the railroads had "no right to show partiality among their customers."[69] The agreements made between Standard Oil and the railroads, principally the Erie, from 1868 to 1872 were mutually advantageous; the former received preferential treatment while the latter allocated the market.[70] The Hepburn hearings fully disclosed these special contracts. They were in no sense discriminatory, because Standard Oil guaranteed minimum volume, furnished tanks to fit on the railroads' wheels, and performed other cost-effective services.

Many years later John D. Rockefeller claimed that the volume and regularity of his firm's freight shipments "should have entitled them to more consideration than the smaller and less regular shippers." Rockefeller always believed that large shippers were entitled to rebates on a cost basis. According to him, those shippers who criticized rebates were those who did not receive them. This view of rebates as a quantity discount was widely held in the business community.[71] The relationship between cost and rate is the entire issue, and it is commonly recognized today that the former justifies the latter.

The South Improvement Company of 1872, organized by several leading refiners including Standard Oil, is perhaps the most infamous rate discrimination scheme. To its outside contemporaries it seemed like robbery.[72] Fred M. Backus, a Cleveland manufacturer of lubricants, condemned it as immoral, because it enriched the strong at the expense of the weak and placed unlimited power in the hands of a small group.[73] John D. Archbold, long after he became a Standard executive, characterized it as "an outrage on the business as a whole that was not included in it."[74] This judgment has been concurred in by those who have examined this particular example of discrimination in detail.[75]

John D. Rockefeller, for his part, was convinced that the South Improvement Company was fair. While the maelstrom whirled about him, Rockefeller confided to his wife: "We will do all right and not be nervous or troubled by what the papers say, by and by when all are through possibly we may briefly respond (though it is not our policy) and leave future events in the business to demonstrate our intentions and plans were just and warranted." He also said, "The fact is that we *did* not contemplate swindling the public in *it* and it is not the business of the public to change our private contracts." (Herein•lies much of the political battle of these and succeeding decades: the question of what is the public's business and what is private.) Even when the South Improvement Company was no longer an issue, Rockefeller privately rose to its (and his own) defense: "I had the plan clearly in mind. It was right. I knew it as a matter of conscience. It was right between me and my God. If I had to do it tomorrow I would do it again the same way—do it a hundred times."[76]

The proceedings of the Hepburn investigation offer a diversity of opinion on every conceivable facet of discrimination.[77] Albert Fink, commissioner of the Trunk Line Association, stated his opposition to rate discrimination not based on cost and expressed his view that all other discriminations were unjust. He went further and contended that every discrimination between shippers was unjust on the face of it until proved otherwise. The common law, according to Fink, prohibited unjust discrimination. Fink's reputation as one of the top dozen railway experts of his day was justly earned by virtue of his experience as both an operating executive and a pool manager. In contrast to Fink, Royal C. Vilas of the Erie pleaded ignorance as to whether discrimination was an abuse or not. He defended discriminatory rates as a competitive necessity and was seconded by George R. Blanchard, assistant to the president of Erie.[78]

One of the accusations hurled at the railroads was that of charging what the traffic would bear. James H. Rutter of the New York Central declared that freight rates varied depending on market conditions, as did other prices, and he therefore defended setting rates as high as possible. Another railroad executive argued in behalf of the value-of-service principle as a proper basis for rates regardless of cost and stated that "we charge merchants the value of what we do for them, rather than what we can get." Since there is no independent way of judging the value of service, the true test is the impact on traffic flow, which ultimately makes charging what the traffic will bear the criterion. Both principles are the same.

Alexander S. Diven, a former Erie officer and director, was on the opposite side of the fence during the Hepburn inquiry. He admitted that although he opposed discriminatory rates, when he had charge of traffic management for Erie, he had made discriminatory rates as a matter of competitive necessity. Diven called for a law to prevent discrimination and said that his actions as an Erie executive were justified because he had been protecting the Erie. He denied that he needed a law to bolster his conscience but instead said: "I didn't make it a matter of conscience." Diven was then asked if he opposed discriminatory rates and if a law was needed to eliminate this, why had he not suggested such a law? Diven's reply is perhaps representative of many men like him: "I can't tell you; we were always a little afraid of introducing legislative interference for fear that it might be carried too far."[79] By establishing a minimum standard of business morality, the law may strengthen the hand of a businessman who would prefer not to invoke a particular competitive practice, but the businessman may be reluctant to invoke the law.

At the outset of the Hepburn investigation, the railroads attempted to keep their books secret on the grounds that their charters were immutable contracts and that therefore the investigation was meaningless.[80] The *New York Evening Post* took the opposite view: "The ground of this mistaken attitude is a false notion of the nature of railroads and their business—the notion that they are private establishments, and their affairs are and ought to be matters of secrecy. Railroads are public establishments."[81]

The concept of a railroad as a public utility was evolving at this time. Although individual states had attempted, ineffectually, to regulate the railroads for several decades, in 1872 Illinois had assumed rate-making power, and its action was upheld by the Supreme Court in *Munn* v. *Illinois* (1877) on the grounds that the railroads were affected with a public interest. The court reasoned, "When, therefore, one devotes his property to a use in which the public has an interest, he, in effect, grants to the public an interest in that use, and must submit to be controlled by the public for the common good."

This decision by no means settled the question irrevocably. One of the continuing questions was the comparability of railroads with other business regarding the prices they charged. Rutter visualized a railroad as a private business comparable to any other,[82] a view concurred in by Leland Stanford who, a few years before the Hepburn investigation, justified rate discrimination and the lack of correspondence between rates and costs as characteristic of private business.[83] Although there were many supporters of this position within the business community, this sentiment was beginning to be challenged by some businessmen. The opposition, however, had not yet developed a coherent argument. A wholesale merchant, in his testimony before the Hepburn committee, endorsed the sale of larger quantities at lower unit prices by a businessman such as himself but wondered whether this should be true of enterprises as the railroads.[84]

The railroads, under duress, made available much information to the Hepburn committee, but Standard Oil, an industrial firm, succeeded in providing little information. When Henry H. Rogers testified that he declined to divulge business secrets, A. Barton Hepburn, the committee chairman, retorted that the committee did not want secrets but the general nature of Standard Oil. John D. Archbold contended that his rates were a secret between him and the railroad and refused to furnish, even privately, the net rate per barrel of refined oil, declaring, "I do not feel it is consistent with the business of my company to expose its business in stating its rates."[85] Since the oil industry was not, according to prevailing opinion, clothed with a public interest, it was not pressed for information as hard as the railroads were.

The mid-nineteenth-century American economy was characterized by price or rate discrimination. Railroad freight rate discrimination was so common that James J. Hill, then a forwarder and later head of the Great Northern, observed in the 1860s, "But the regular rate can hardly be said to be established."[86] In assessing this competitive tactic, prevalent throughout the economy, we must consider its pervasiveness and the fact that certain types of discrimination as between persons or shippers now have legal standing under public supervision; specific practices once condemned as discriminatory are now acceptable. Contrary to the wishes of some ill-informed critics a century ago, the railroads have never been compelled to adhere to the pricing policies of the post office. Carriers are, however, required to demonstrate that discrimination is based on cost differentials rather than on sheer bargaining skill or power; the unitized train illustrates the advantage that accrues to a shipper who can combine enough volume in a single shipment.

Freight rate discrimination increasingly came under fire from those shippers who were not beneficiaries of the system and particularly those in industries in which freight cost was vital. Such shippers founded protest organizations and mounted an aggressive propaganda campaign aimed at the general public with an eye toward the passage of legislation. With *Munn* v. *Illinois* in 1877, the conclusion of the Hepburn inquiry in 1879, and the wide press coverage accorded its hearings, the idea that the railroads, clothed with a public interest, could not morally dispense favors had come to the fore and garnered limited acceptance by 1880 but as yet had not gained the status of anything remotely approaching the universalistic ethic.

STOCK WATERING

Stock watering, a feature of corporate life in this period, can be defined as an increase in par or nominal capitalization without a commensurate increase in physical assets. The problem is that the value of any enterprise, incorporated or not, depends on its earning capacity, and earning capacity determines the market value of a corporation's securities. Hence the practice of watered stock commonly implies the deception of investors and the public.

People living at the time clung tenaciously to a trinity of beliefs: physical assets as a determinant of value, par value, and the idea that equity securities could have an intrinsic value long after such notions should have been discarded. The grip of the dead hand of the past could not be broken until the twentieth century when stock watering was finally seen to be an empty, sterile, and jejune concept.

The railroads, as they so often did in matters of this sort, led the way. The first opportunity for stock watering occurred with a railroad's construction. The use of an inside construction company was an easy way of injecting water into the construction account of a railroad, since then the railroad would appear to cost as much as its capitalization.[87] Securities could be issued to represent the nominal cost of construction even though it might be excessive. Insiders in this arrangement could be simultaneously inefficient and fraudulent. Frequently all of the stock was water and was paid to the contractor or other insiders.[88] Such stock was valueless until the road was built. If a contractor took stock in payment or partial payment, he was gambling that the road would be profitable enough for him to sell his shares at a profit or hold them, as he saw fit. The problem arose for purchasers of the stock, since they might not know that they were buying stock that was, and might remain, valueless.

Later opportunities for stock watering also existed. One illustration will suffice. The consolidation of the New York Central in 1853, legislatively sanctioned by the state of New York, involved watered stock, because the whole was greater than the sum of all its parts. No one at the consolidation convention objected to the use of it; the arguments dealt with the relative amounts for each of the companies that participated in the consolidation.[89] Water again was added during the consolidation of the Central and Hudson River Railroad. Vanderbilt took control of the New York Central in 1867; and the next year the Central, before it merged with the Hudson River, issued the "80 per cent certificates of indebtedness," which represented an increase in capitalization.[90] The New York Central and the Hudson River railroads were consolidated in 1869, and certificates were issued representing nothing except the future profit expectations of the entrepreneurs, all of which were fully realized.

Not only investors but the public at large had an interest in stock of this sort because of the link between capitalization, earning capacity, and rates. As early as 1853, Henry Varnum Poor expressed his opposition to stock watering. Poor specifically objected to the New York Central consolidation of that year as a burden on the customer by justifying increased rates and profits.[91] Those who participated in the consolidation, conversely, thought that the new capitalization was fair and reasonable. They held that the watered stock represented the market value based on earning power rather than water in excess of capitalization cost because the consolidated profits of the previous year (1852) were about 7 percent (the then legal rate of interest) on the new capitalization.[92]

According to the defenders of watered stock, its existence was of no consequence to the public because competition fixed the level of rates and thereby fixed earning power and capitalization. The critics contended that railroad rates were not fixed by competition, at least not in the traditional sense of many buyers and many sellers, and that since earning power could not be derived indirectly from competition, it had to be derived from something else—actual investment.

It was thus the relation of capitalization, rates, and earning power or rates of profit that was the crux of the agitation, and the entire subject was related to both competition and regulation. Not until the Valuation Act of 1913 and the Transportation Act of 1920—by severing the ostensible connection between capitalization and rates—did watered stock regarding railroads become a dead issue.

Edwin D. Worcester, who had joined the New York Central when it was organized in 1853 and was its treasurer in 1869 and its secretary in 1879, explained before the Hepburn committee how the watered stock was added during the consolidation. According to his recollection the Consolidation Act authorized the two railroads to consolidate, and the capital stock of the consolidated company was fixed at an amount well in excess of the sum of the capitals of the two separate companies.[93] The capitalization therefore was more closely related to future earning capacity than to past investment.

Since the New York Central was owned to such a large extent by the Vanderbilts, one might inquire as to why stock watering was employed at all. The relation of capitalization (physical or water), rates, and profits or dividends provided the answer. The New York general railroad law of 1850 placed a limit on the earnings of railroads to 10 percent on actual cost, using capitalization as the basis of computation. Therefore, stock watering, rather than defrauding investors, constituted an evasion of the spirit of the law for it reduced the apparent rate of profit.

Despite the depression of 1873, and while the Erie was bankrupt, the Central paid its regular 8 percent divident on the larger capitalization as it had on the smaller, or about 32 percent on its actual cash investment.[94] The New York merchants charged that the necessity of paying a return on watered capitalization explained the high freight rates, while the railroad retorted that capitalization was not related to rates. The rates were set, in effect, by the costs of marginal lines—in New York State, the Erie—and the New

York Central thus made large economic "rents'" flowing from its superb low-cost *route*. Vanderbilt and Jewett in the Joint Letter submitted to the Hepburn committee denied that rates were set so as to sustain a fictitious capital.[95] "Competition fixes rates without regard to the amount of any company's stocks or bonds," they stated. As if in verification of this, they cited the existence of the five trunk lines east from Chicago.[96] However, pooling, which was being used more extensively year by year, negated competition and thus removed the incentive for reasonable rates, leaving in its wake the ability, at intervals at least, to set rates high enough to enable a railroad to pay dividends on capitalization, whether watered or not.

The subject of stock watering dominated and enlivened the public interest during this era. Commodore Cornelius Vanderbilt rebutted those who criticized his role in the merger of the New York Central and Hudson River railroads. He argued that the increase in capitalization was justified by the gain in earnings and that earnings, not assets, were the proper basis of capitalization.[97] This is the essence of the issue, and today authorities would concur. Agreeing with Vanderbilt, Hugh Jewett of the Erie defended the issuance of watered stock if it was based on earnings. William H. Vanderbilt, the son of the Commodore, told the Hepburn committee that the stock watering related to the consolidation represented the earnings of the road that the stockholders ought to have had earlier.[98]

Businessmen engaged in manufacturing were also interested in the question of the proper basis of capitalization. In the annual report of the Trenton Iron Company of 1853, Abram Hewitt, an insider, noted that the business was valued on a cost basis, which included nothing for experience, skill, or goodwill. He also observed that managerial skill and experience had not been charged to the construction account: "I believe that it is a low estimate to value this experience, skill and business connection at 50 per cent of the whole cost of the property."[99] Contemporaries did not distinguish between competitive conditions in the railroads and the iron industry, nor did they clearly perceive the difference between the railroads—which were subject to some sort of regulation concerning stock watering, however rudimentary or ineptly administered—and the iron industry, in which capitalization was not regulated at all. They did understand that railroads were not strictly private; the New York law of 1850 explicitly linked the rate of return to actual cost and therefore implicitly to capitalization, thereby attempting to prevent stock watering and higher freight and passenger rates. Hence, it can be seen that capitalization or stock watering, especially because of its presumed connection to profits and rates, was by no means an easy question to resolve. More was heard of it later, and during the eighties and nineties the Supreme Court whittled away at the scope of the principle e-nunciated in *Munn* v. *Illinois*.

However much the argument that earning power should be a determinant of capitalization may have appealed to those railroad managers who contended that other types of business were anal-ogous, outsiders challenged the validity of increased capitalization if unrelated to actual cost. By using the rate of return to set limits on earnings and rates, the public acknowledged that competition, while present, differed in transportation from what prevailed in the rest of the economy and therefore could not properly protect the public. Since this was an important issue to the electorate, as early as 1839 the states instituted regulatory commissions and then broadened their power during the 1870s. This marked the inception of the public utility concept, which rested on the belief that certain goods and services are vital to the community and therefore should be subject to regulation.

The morality of stock watering was questioned both by investors as it affected the market price of a security and the expectation of future earnings as well as by the public as it affected the price of a product or service. The railroads were uniquely the concern of society since the more or less absolute right of other sectors of the economy to act as they pleased was widely recognized. The public manifested its concern about stock watering probably because of the presumably pragmatic connection between it, capitalization, the rate of return, and the rate level. Investors, and particularly the public, increasingly ventilated the moral issue inherent in stock watering, but at times with more heat than light in what was really a meaningless controversy, and there was little perceptible alteration in either action or attitude.

FINANCIAL REPORTING

In financial reporting, neither theory nor practice was adequate to cope with the problems of the new era. Financial reports were used by those who prepared them and no others. Thus, while they may have been defective and inaccurate as a guide to action, they had little occasion to be deliberately misleading. The railroads, as the first large-scale, widely-held enterprises, were the first to contend with the task of developing and applying generally accepted accounting principles to such new situations as fixed assets, which were a significant share of total assets, the meaning of capitalization, and the nature of profit. Not only the owner-managers, insiders, had a vested interest in such matters; other investors and the public generally were equally concerned.

In this epoch, railroad accounting—and accounting in general, for that matter—frequently offered a deceptive statement of the condition of the enterprise. Comparisons of financial conditions among railroads were not possible until the Massachusetts law of 1876 required uniform accounting.[100] (This matter was not resolved nationally until the Hepburn Act of 1906.) Also, until the Interstate Commerce Commission ruling of 1907 instituted depreciation accounting, the practice of replacement accounting was almost universal. Replacement accounting meant that equipment replacements were charged to current operating expenses at the time expenditures were made, and no entry ever appeared in the capital account. Replacement accounting, thoroughly legitimate and still practiced for some purposes, may have conveyed a misleading impression of the financial condition of the enterprise. On the other hand, it has been acceptable to charge trackage costs to earnings at the time the work was performed since the Supreme Court decision in 1879 that capital improvements might "in good faith be charged to earnings." As experience was acquired in coping with the complex problems of accounting for large-scale, multiplant organizations, the practitioners became increasingly adept. However, the difficulty was compounded both by the tradition of privacy that enveloped and protected every business and by the apprenticeship method of transmitting such expertise as had been acquired.

Management manipulated the construction account both unintentionally and intentionally. A high rate of profit could be reduced by increasing the construction account, because the rate of profit was based on the relationship between the amount of profit and capitalization or construction. Reducing the rate of profit would justify it and, therefore, the rate level. Since the public tended to want lower rates, the profitable railroads avoided rate decreases by closing the construction account and putting construction items into the operating expense account. Marginal roads, in order to look better, did the opposite; they padded the construction account. For example, transferring an item from the expense account to the construction account decreased expenses and offered the illusion of increased earnings. Each railroad manipulated its financial reports in accordance with its own financial exigencies, making comparison of costs and rates impossible. The universalistic ethic tolerated juggling since financial reports were hardly comprehensible to the average layman, and, although objections were raised from time to time, it is probable that the subject was too technical to arouse the uninitiated or those not directly affected.

Henry Varnum Poor, a competent spokesman for the investor, objected to the abuse of the construction account and called for better accounting in the 1850s. He condemned the Michigan Central in 1854 and 1855 for adding to its construction account while doing no construction. In addition, this railroad continued to pay dividends, which it had not earned, but it concealed this from the public, because it failed to include depreciation. Poor also criticized the Erie Railroad in 1853 and 1854 for poor accounting practices, alleging that the accounts were such that they could be manipulated to hide incompetence or fraud.[101]

Poor's complaints concerning the Erie's accounting were not advanced without good reason. In 1854 it became known that the financial report contained discrepancies. An investigatory committee was appointed by the directors, and it was expected that its report would be available before the annual stockholders' meeting, but instead it was released just after. The report revealed that the floating debt was understated by over a million dollars; this had the effect of overstating earnings.[102]

There is no indication whether specific accounting practices were the result of ignorance or a deliberate attempt to deceive. In an enterprise with few owners, the purpose of the financial reports was to provide the insiders with a statement of condition; it rarely had a larger purpose. When the enterprise became larger, numerous outsiders had an interest in the financial reports. For this reason such complaints as were registered by minority stockholders or the general public were directed at both competence and morality, since the quality of financial reports was only beginning to be perceived as a moral issue.

Financial reporting is by no means even now universally consistent, and in that day the optional element was considerable. John Murray Forbes directed the auditor of the Burlington: "It is clear to me that in the present temper of public opinion it is expedient to err on the safe side if either way, namely by rather overloading expenses than overloading construction. The latter fault strikes at the root of *confidence*."[103] This short statement illustrates three key points: the discretionary power of management in its financial reporting practices, the role of the public in influencing management, and the importance of the construction account.

The stockholders' report for the Erie in 1872 included legal expenses under the construction heading. In a footnote to the report, the auditor commented: "The propriety of putting this item in the construction account is questionable, but it was so arranged by the former administration."[104] The auditor was aware that this was a dubious practice, and he also recognized that his readers would look askance at it. But Hugh Jewett argued before the Hepburn committee that the construction account had to be used to absorb all sorts of charges because there was no other place to put them.[105] Although this statement could be taken at face value— the state of accounting was almost primitive—it should not be. Simon Sterne, counsel of the Hepburn committee, reminded members that the New York general railroad law of 1850 restricted railroads to profits of 10 percent on invested capital actually expended in construction. This law therefore induced an inflated construction account.[106]

The profit and loss account could also be manipulated deliberately. The auditor of the Erie resigned in 1874, stating correctly that the report for the 1873 fiscal year was false, that the president of the road was aware of this, that the floating debt was more than twice as much as the report showed, and that the dividend paid in 1873 had not been earned, although the accounts had been altered to show that it had.[107] Similarly, the Wabash Railroad, under the management of Jay Gould, publicly reported a profit of $168,000 for 1877, but in a lawsuit soon after, the treasurer revealed a deficit of $570,000.[108] The reasons for overstating profits included stock market speculation and the maintenance of existing management control.

Some men were quite concerned about the reliability of the accounts of companies with which they either were or might be involved. When Edward Atkinson, a textile manufacturer, was invited to join the board of directors of the Little Rock and Fort Smith Railroad, he examined the railroad's financial statements. But they did not satisfy him, and he never went on the board.[109] As he wrote before he made his decision:

I shall be glad of any information on the subject, but of one thing you may be assured, if I become a director in the Little Rock and Fort Smith Railroad, no payment, deposit, or other expenditure will be made by my consent that is not entered on the books of the company as paid to certain persons thereon named for purposes thereon designated. From the date that I enter on the duties, until I go out, every transaction must be open, clean and of record.[110]

A man like Atkinson was a potential source of internal change, because he recognized that moral issues were involved.

The accounting practices of the period were inconsistent, and the public reports frequently were worse than useless. Even the reports filed by the railroads with public supervisory agencies were not very useful because the state failed to ask for proper information, which made evasion and concealment by insiders simple. Accounting was still in the process of evolving from the bookkeeping techniques appropriate to small-scale, closely-held business enterprise. Still, change, moral as well as technical, was instigated. Massachusetts, a state with numerous highly regarded financial institutions, acted in 1876 to require uniform financial reporting for railroads. Henry Varnum Poor continued to heap scorn on those who dealt falsely with the investing public. Lawsuits instituted by dissident stockholders compelled management to provide trustworthy information. And some businessmen, such as Edward Atkinson, demanded honesty of themselves and others. What was acceptable at the beginning of the period would no longer pass muster at the end.

New fortunes of an unprecedented magnitude were achieved between the 1840s and 1870s during the phenomenal development of industrial America. Some men deplored the wealth and power of the captains of industry on general principles, while others contended that they flourished because of their business immorality. The dynamism of the economy was matched by far-reaching changes in its business morality.

Some of the change in morality was internally generated. Often the conflict between dissident stockholders and management was won by stockholders, and when they came into control, they instituted the system that they had advocated. Some of the changes came about because new protective systems were devised that all but eliminated certain forms of business behavior. The use of a separate stock register, for example, made the issuance of fraudulent stock so obvious that those who once might have been tempted either abandoned such ideas completely or else sought another, if still immoral, device.

There is evidence that businessmen during this period were concerned with questions of the morality of business behavior. Outsiders such as the press (itself a business enterprise) publicized and commented on the actions of other businessmen; and government, through legislative investigations, legislation, and regulatory commissions, set a new standard, since the law crystallized morality. At the same time, some businessmen evaded laws, which they regarded as obstacles to overcome.

There was a greater awareness of the moral implications of business behavior at the end of the period than at the beginning. The existence of larger enterprises using the corporate form of organization, with many stockholders and having a broader impact on more people, required that some businessmen explain their actions to themselves and to others.

The mere fact that a businessman had to submit an annual report to his stockholders—as more and more did throughout this period—compelled him to think about matters that he might previously have taken for granted and forced him to develop a justification for his actions. This very process caused individuals to examine why they made their decisions. On the other hand and pushing in a contrary direction, the newly sprung corporation created a shield of anonymity that contributed to corporate managers' feeling less personal responsibility for their actions.

This era ended on a somewhat higher plane than it had begun on. Both the Burlington revolution of 1875 and the Hepburn inquiry vindicated the New York railroads on several matters, and these had effects throughout the country. The early conflict-of-interest situations had generally been eliminated, although there were some exceptions. As an aftermath of this investigation, in 1880 the New York legislature passed laws regulating the manner in which capital stock could be increased, as well as the consolidation of railroads, and revised the requirements for the reports that were to be filed with the state. Moderate action against both personal and place discrimination was defeated, however.[111] On some points legislators modified the law in order to express new convictions as to what constituted moral behavior, thereby providing businessmen with guidance.

Businessmen themselves had an image of their peers that was not at all flattering. "I fear you hit it too correctly when you said that possibly the morality of railroad managers was of too low a grade to expect honesty and maintenance of good faith," one wrote his superior.[112] Even such a seemingly universalistic principle as the sanctity of contract could not always be relied on; and when some men adhered to the terms of an unfavorable contract, it was for reasons of policy as much as of principle. Railroad men felt that business had a particularistic code and the public another, and that the public did not understand the necessity of certain practices.[113] This attitude may help to explain the public antagonism that the railroads confronted.

A businessman may well have been insensitive to the moral implications of a particular action and, from his vantage point, he may not have seen what was perfectly obvious to his critics. Quite possibly there was no source of criticism whose right to criticize he would acknowledge. The adage "business is business" separated business ethics from the rest of the world and its morality. Religion, a source that might have been expected to provide some ethical guidance, did not. For some businessmen, religion was a private matter without business implications. Even those who have been labeled robber barons in their public lives were models of rectitude and stern religious faith in their private lives.

The views of businessmen on general matters of business morality are of considerable interest because of their broad range. One question concerned to whom (or to what) one should be loyal. William Pitt Shearman, treasurer and assistant to the receiver of Erie, was dismissed from these positions in 1878 by Hugh Jewett. Jewett charged Shearman with disloyalty, but Shearman claimed that he was dismissed only because he would not approve certain accounting practices. Some years later Shearman informed the author of a history of the Erie: "If any action I ever took while connected with the Jewett management could be called disloyalty it thus became all the greater an act of loyalty to the true interests of the company.[114] Who has the right to define the true interests of a company or a state is a perplexing dilemma; definitions may vary according to point of view.

Critics lamented that no effective code of business ethics existed. Charles Francis Adams, Jr., a knowledgeable observer, charged in 1869 in an influential magazine that American society, in weighing conflicting values, honored wealth more than honesty: "Failure seems to be regarded as the one unpardonable crime, success as the all-redeeming virtue, the acquisition of wealth as the single worthy aim of life."[115] Adams, who had not yet embarked on his career as railroad regulator and manager, remained a marginal man, out of tune with his times.

Some well-informed men voiced strong views on the ethics of business generally. Abraham Wolff, a partner in the prestigious and honorable firm of Kuhn, Loeb & Company, expressed doubt as to the existence of business morality. Simon Sterne, no doubt reasoning from such statements as well as from five thousand pages of testimony before the Hepburn committee, denied that railway managers were governed by ordinary universalistic moral principles.[116]

On the other hand, some businessmen thought large-scale corporations should be as moral in their behavior as individuals. Hugh Jewett of the Erie informed his inquisitors that "no corporation is justified in doing an unlawful act . . . and a railroad company must be managed within the law." Thomas Dickson of the Delaware & Hudson addressed himself to this point and to another closely related one—corporate business as differentiated from any other business. He advised the Hepburn committee, "I regard any business that is conducted on business principles, conducted in the same manner as an individual should conduct his own private business; I think the idea that corporations can be managed differently from the way individuals conduct their own business is a delusion."[117]

It was, and is, this delusion that has been offered as an explanation for some business behavior. Just as the nation-state came to command the whole of a man's loyalty, and also his moral judgment, so perhaps this is equally true of the enterprise. For some time, the exact role of the corporation as a social institution was a matter of debate. Some businessmen acted on behalf of their corporations in a manner more akin to the way in which men acted on behalf of the state rather than on their own behalf. A man might practice deception for the benefit of his enterprise with the same lack of hesitation that a diplomat might lie for the good of his country.

3 THE FEDERAL GOVERNMENT AS REGULATOR 1880~1900

The most striking development during the last two decades of the nineteenth century was the intrusion of the federal government into the realm of business morality. As government proscribed some practices and prescribed others, it gradually asserted its authority to set higher and universalistic moral as well as legal standards of business behavior. Some individual states had engaged in this sort of activity earlier, but as the economy became increasingly less parochial, the maladies ceased to be amenable to local remedies.

Federal intervention was halting and stumbling, but, it was a decisive beginning; once embarked on this course, the nation never turned back. Demands from railroads, shippers, and the general public, each with its own motivations, culminated in an act to regulate commerce, otherwise known as the Interstate Commerce Act of 1887, which brought administrative agencies into being. A decade or more of experience with state action and agitation by pressure groups contributed to thrusting regulation on the federal government. Finally, public pressure induced the enactment of other basic laws, and the pressure of law and opinion became strong enough to impair business unanimity on many ethical issues.

Response to popular clamor against business bigness and power, as well as an extension of the common law against monopoly, eventuated in an Act to Protect Trade and Commerce Against Unlawful Restraints and Monopoly, commonly known as the

Sherman Antitrust Act of 1890. Here, too, the moral lesson was drawn with increasing clarity: the act's very phrase "restraint of trade" is laden with moral overtones. Neither of these laws was wholly effective in its professed purpose during the period at hand, but they constituted landmarks and established the precedents upon which similar and later legislation was enacted.

CONFLICT OF INTEREST

The forms taken by the conflict of interest during this period were essentially unchanged from the earlier part of the century. In the early stage, when railroad builders lacked capital, knowledge, equipment, and experience, they used separate construction companies. Later, as they accumulated both capital and experience, many corporations began to serve as their own contractors, with no attempt to conceal or to misrepresent. In the earlier period, most investors had been opportunistic; they were not specializing businessmen. At that time, every opportunity to make money was still regarded as legitimate, and recognition that a conflict of interest was improper emerged only from the continued clash of interests and ideas. The ripple effect of the revolution of 1875 in the Burlington as yet had only a limited effect.

Grenville M. Dodge, one of the outstanding railroad construction men, in his relations with the Fort Worth and Denver City (later part of the Burlington system), acted in a dual and conflicting capacity both as seller and buyer in the same transactions, but he always made clear in what capacity he was acting. In 1886, Dodge functioned as a salaried official and did some railroad construction at cost plus his compensation. This applied only to a limited amount of construction; in the same year, Dodge organized an inside construction company to do a major project for the Fort Worth and Denver. Dodge's contemporaries were generally unconcerned with the morality of his behavior and allowed him to select his method as he saw fit; they judged the ends, not the means.[1]

The past, as regards conflict of interest, was not completely dead, as a series of incidents graphically demonstrates. Benjamin Franklin Yoakum, chairman of the board of the St. Louis and San Francisco (Frisco) Railway, participated in the construction of certain subsidiary lines. He invested his own money, formed an inside construction company to finance and construct the line and later sold the property to the parent company.[2] Nevertheless, there were indications of a growing awareness of the moral problems of conflict of interest. According to Joseph W. Reinhart, president of the Santa Fe in 1894, the road had been buying oil from a director, Alden Speare. Reinhart stopped this practice and purchased directly from Standard Oil for less money, informing Speare that directors could not trade with the railroad.[3]

Conflict-of-interest situations occurred in industry in a variety of ways. When Bucyrus-Erie, manufacturer of excavating machinery, went into receivership in 1895, one of the directors proposed himself as receiver, although indirectly he was the principal creditor of the company. Another director objected:

Almost all of the available accounts were assigned either to your mother or to Walter [brother of the correspondent], and [the fact] that consequently it would be your duty to apply almost all of the prospective collections to the retirement of your own debts, would seem to constitute an insuperable obstacle to your taking the position.[4]

This was a relatively small business, and those concerned wanted a friendly receiver but not one who might be guilty of favoritism.

Standard Oil was one of the largest American manufacturers during this period. Its ownership and management were identical for all practical purposes, and this fact may well have removed the motivation for certain practices in which others indulged. Nevertheless, a Standard leader probably did act improperly. In 1881 Colonel W. P. Thompson, a Standard Oil executive, suspected that independent oil was going into the territory of Chess, Carley & Company, a marketing subsidiary half owned by Standard, with the connivance of F. B. Carley, who had presumably made a deal to his own advantage and contrary to Standard's general interests. However, in that same year its noted attorney, S. C. T. Dodd, declined to become an owner of consequence (through a kind of stock option plan, which would have made him wealthy) so that he could render the most objective service as counsel. Similarly, Charles Lockhart, a Standard Oil manager, declined to serve on the Cooperage Supply Committee in 1882 because he had a personal interest in a firm that sold cooperage supplies; he elected to maintain that relation rather than subordinate it to Standard's welfare.[5]

Sometimes the corporate interest triumphed over individual interests. In 1892, Henry H. Rogers and William Rockefeller competed with J. Edward Addicks in the field of water gas, which used naphtha as a base. Addicks approached a Standard executive, Charles M. Higgins, to buy oil. Higgins was aware of Roger's potential opposition to the deal but thought Standard could use the profit from any large order. Higgins consulted colleagues John D. Archbold and W. H. Tilford, and they agreed to sell. As Higgins recalled the episode many years later, Archbold told him, "I think it is a-very-good deal you have made." But Rogers was angry: I don't understand this fool transaction." He was silenced by Higgins's statement, "If you will examine the price paid the Standard I think you will agree that it was a very profitable transaction."[6]

Andrew Carnegie and Henry Clay Frick provided another example of intrafirm disagreement on a question involving conflict of interest, this time in a firm with only a few owners. The two men and their firms joined forces in 1882; Carnegie made steel and bought coke, and Frick produced and sold coke. Carnegie Steel bought its coke from the Frick Coke Company at below market prices, to the disadvantage of the minority stockholders in the latter company. These two interrelated companies had agreed about the price of coke for ten years before matters came to a head. Carnegie directly owned 25 percent in the H. C. Frick Coke Company and indirectly (through the Carnegie Steel Company) had majority control of the coke concern; Frick owned 23 percent (others owned the remainder). And thus in case of conflict between the coke company and its most important customer, "the customer was always right." Carnegie Steel wanted a special price on coke, but Frick Coke wanted the price high enough so as to avoid challenge by the minority stockholders. In 1899 Frick asked the directors of Carnegie Steel, "Why should he [Carnegie] whose chief interest is larger in steel than it is in coke, insist on fixing the price which the Steel Company should pay for their coke?"[7] Because of his protests against the conflict of interest between Carnegie directly as buyer and indirectly as seller in a closely-held company, and for other reasons, Frick was ultimately and acrimoniously forced out of the Carnegie Steel Company.[8]

Leaders of some railroads made most of their money not from dividends but rather from auxiliary enterprises fed by the major railroad company.[9] The possibilities included not only the inside construction company but also land and town-site operations, special rates for enterprises or localities in which insiders were interested, fast freight lines, buying from or selling to the railroad, or use of inside information for speculation. Such men had been schooled in an age of small owner-managed enterprises and tended to invest in auxiliary enterprises as a matter of course. They thought of themselves more as general entrepreneurs and less as railroad men alone. But over time, these men began to consider themselves more and more as railroad men and protect their railroad as an enterprise against the depredations of those who sought to exploit it for their personal gain. In 1876 the Louisville & Nashville prohibited conflict of interest, and a decade later Milton H. Smith, its president, reminded his directors that "the difference between the company's property and that of the individual officers and employees has been clearly established. . . . [They] clearly understand that their time belongs to the company, and that they will not be permitted to have individual interests, or engage in enterprises on their personal account that can in any way conflict with the interests of the company."[10]

By this time attitudes on the question of conflict of interest had clarified considerably. William Taussig, president of the St. Louis Terminal Railroad Association, commented in 1898, "Thus it will be seen how elastic, in recent times, the conscience of the average railroad officer has been, and how, unconscious almost of doing any wrong, he took advantage of his position often to the disadvantage of the interest entrusted to him, to enrich himself." He noted that with the exception of the roads east of the Appalachians and some others, railroads, and especially branches, constructed in this period frequently used inside construction companies: "On their face and on strict principles of honesty, such acts are wrong and improper. If there is profit in the transaction, it belongs to the company, if there is risk of loss, the project should not be undertaken."[11] Taussig thus focused sharply on the moral issue and succeeded in obtaining a clear image.

Similarly, T. Jefferson Coolidge, a Boston capitalist, was quite unlike the typical officer and director who used his inside position for speculation. Coolidge was elected president and director of the Santa Fe in 1880 but resigned both offices in 1881, because, as he recollected years later, "I found the work not only fatiguing but unprofitable, because as director and president I felt that my duty to my *cestuis que trust*, the shareholders, prevented me from taking advantage of any facts not known to all, and cut me off from speculations which might have been advantageous. I resigned as soon as I could."[12]

A few years later the Santa Fe told its stockholders, "Every mile of our new roads has been built by the Company itself: and no Construction Company has been interposed to increase their cost, thus securing to our stockholders the actual value of every dollar which has been expended upon their property."[13] The mere inclusion of such a statement in a report to stockholders testifies that conflict of interest had become a matter of enough concern to the stockholders of a major railroad so that management deemed it desirable to communicate its position.

Conflict of interest was a form of business behavior that had not yet been appreciably affected by the action of government. The cause of reform apparently emanated from the notions of some men about business morality, coupled with a growing recognition of what would be tolerated by the increasingly sophisticated small investors in the capital market; together the insiders and outsiders succeeded in raising business morality. Conflict of interest was a business practice and a moral standard in the process of evolution. Some businessmen were pointing to changes in their business practices with pride; simultaneously others were alarmed at the changes. Thus the old and the new coexisted, but the shape of the future was foreshadowed.

Although there was a change over time, there continued to be a range of action and opinion among the various roads and within the same road. When the Denver, Texas and Fort Worth was organized in 1887, Grenville M. Dodge, a large owner of construction company stock, insisted to a director that no one on the railway's board should hold construction company stock in his own name. But Dodge's solution—"If he wants it he must put it in another's name"—was to evade the moral principle of business behavior.[14] Nevertheless there is cognizance that a principle exists. In 1893 one executive of the Gulf-to-Rockies system (of which the Denver, Texas and Fort Worth became a part) advised another executive to sell his coal business. The latter did not, but even the former waited until 1898 to sell his own.

In that same year Dodge moralized to a third executive that "parties in charge of railways are liable to criticism no matter how fairly they may try to act where interests are conflicting."[15] He clearly recognized the issue, but the impetus for action was external to the individual who began with self-interest as a guide to action. There was a considerable lapse of time between knowing the right and doing the right.

In addition, men were of mixed minds about conflict of interest behavior. Some men in the Land Department of the Northern Pacific colluded with buyers so that the buyer would be able to buy land at the minimum price and split the profits of the subsequent resale with the railroad employee. The president complained to the land commissioner: "You must see that the outside speculation of the Officer is really in conflict with his duties to the Company. He is really seller and purchaser both."[16] When some Northern Pacific officers used their inside knowledge of the railroad's plans to buy land with the intention of reselling to the railroad, they were told to sell it at cost or face dismissal.[17] But Henry Villard, president of the Northern Pacific, was more ambivalent. Although by 1883 the universalistic code was opposing inside construction companies, he invited a banking firm to participate in such a contract.[18] On the other hand, he wrote a relative, "I cannot afford to make myself a party in interest in real estate operations which might bring me in conflict with my duties as head of N. P. [Northern Pacific]."[19] The worst case of conflict of interest on the Northern Pacific (a wretchedly administered enterprise) was the Northern Pacific's acquisition, while under Villard's control and despite the expressed opposition of two Northern Pacific vice-presidents, of the Wisconsin Central.[20]

The president of the Illinois Central, in order to avoid the implication of conflict of interest, handled a land transaction quite openly.
A tract of property was offered for sale. He asked a vice-president
to place the matter before the directors with the understanding
that he, the president, would buy it if the railroad did not.[21]

Some executives were more concerned with public reaction
than with the impropriety of an act. "On general principles," one
informed a fellow executive, "I do not believe in R. R. officials
being interested in enterprises along the line of their Road, as it
gives an opportunity to say that they favor their concerns."[22] In
another letter on the same subject a few years later he wrote: "It is
bad enough as it is to have the Directors of our Company interested
in business matters upon our line."[23]

In comparison to his contemporaries, John Murray Forbes, a
dominant figure in the Burlington, was quite different. He wrote
to an executive of the Rock Island when he proposed an alliance
between their two roads affirming with approval his belief that
both roads had "long been managed by Directors who own the
stock and look after it somewhat as men do their own business."[24]
Still, he commented to a close associate:

Vanderbilt or Gould have a great advantage over us in these stock
operations—they can buy and sell millions of company stock as if it were
their own. We have never done it . . . and while I agree that it might be
legitimately done in this case under cover of the Council Bluffs trade I
fear the effect of it, especially as I know how such operations have always
been looked upon in Boston.

Thus, although many historians have frequently presented him
without blemish, Thomas Cochran provides an alternate view:
"While Forbes also may have been guided by internal sanctions it
is interesting to note that what the financers of Boston would
think (their sanctioning ideas of a proper social role) is given as
the major reason for refraining from such speculation."[25]

Charles Elliott Perkins, Forbes's protégé, echoed him brilliantly.
He informed another official of the Burlington that neither he nor
his correspondent could buy some available coal land because
of its value to the Burlington and their connections with it. There-

fore, either the railroad itself or individuals not connected with it
would have to buy the land.[26] He was even more explicit to some-
one else: "The smallest kind of interest in a coal mine would be
objectionable, while a much larger relative interest in a bank
would not."[27] With obvious pride he was able to gloat to his
mentor: "CB&Q officials don't do what *it is said* they do on most
roads and that is to make money out of side shows."[28]

In industry as well as in railroads, insiders occasionally acted to
the detriment of others. Although the U.S. Industrial Commission
(1900–1902) primarily investigated monopolies and combinations, its nineteen volumes of testimony offer a wealth of in-
valuable material about business methods and policies, including
conflict of interest. Francis Lynde Stetson, a highly successful
corporation lawyer, in his testimony before the Industrial Commission, acknowledged that directors may act in their own interest
and not those of the stockholders. However, he contended that
directors were generally faithful, in spite of their private interests,
to the interests of the stockholders and their freedom of action
should be maintained to promote efficiency. Stetson felt that
limitation by law was unwise because efficiency would be lost.[29]
Even the mere mention of limitation by law brought to the fore
both the recognition of the impropriety of conflict of interest and
the possibility that such a practice was amenable to legal restriction.

When a meat packer was confronted by the high price charged
for salt by the National Salt Company, he and others organized a
company to supply himself and other local packers and sell the
surplus. But he denied that conflict of interest existed or that his
company, the Empire State Salt Company, accorded the owners
as insiders a favored price.

> We have to pay the market price to our [Empire State Salt] Company.
> Of course there are other stockholders, and it would not be fair to them if
> we got our salt at cost and the other stockholders did not get any dividend.
> We agreed to pay the market price for the salt we buy of our company.
> Then the other stockholders have an equal chance at the profits with us.[30]

Charles M. Schwab, president of United States Steel and before
that an associate of Andrew Carnegie, related to the same audience,

the Industrial Commission, the reasons for the creation of the
Carnegie Company (a closely-held concern dominated by its name-
sake). Carnegie had begun with Carnegie Steel and then added
more partnerships for different functions.

One of the chief reasons for that was Mr. Carnegie's idea that a partner
in the coke interest, for example, should not have a greater interest in
coke than he had in steel, as it might affect the contracts between the
two companies; or that a partner should not have a greater interest
in shipping than in the steel company; so he put these interests all into one
company, so that each partner's interest was a whole.[31]

The contrast between this procedure and that pursued in many of
the railroads is quite striking. For reasons of purely personal profit,
Carnegie adopted a method of organization designed to protect
him by eliminating conflict of interest at the highest level.

Edward Dean Adams, president of the Cataract Construction
Company (Niagara Falls), handled the conflict-of-interest issue in
an unusual way. He resigned from the board of directors of the
Edison Illuminating Company "in order to remove all questions of
personal interest which might restrict the freedom with which
information might otherwise be supplied . . . [because he anticipated
that] questions would arise regarding electrical transmission
particularly as to the use of direct or alternating current."[32] Unlike
many of his contemporaries, he yielded the opportunity to take
special advantage of his position.

Although insiders continued to apply different standards of
behavior to outsiders and to take advantage of their position at the
expense of outsiders, the incidence of such acts continued to
decrease; moreover, there was ample evidence of a dialogue among
those concerned. The emergence of the widely-held corporation
and the separation of ownership from management facilitated the
conflict of interest but at the same time was accompanied by
a parallel development, the burgeoning of numerous small and
ever more knowledgeable investors. The result was a wide and
shifting range of behavior and consequently a conflict of values.
In this conflict, the universalistic triumphed over the particularistic
values of the insider. Most individuals could not help but be

aware of the approved behavior, and it became less possible for them to plead ignorance. In this fashion the standard of business morality as applied to conflict of interest was raised.

RESTRAINT OF TRADE

As the nineteenth century drew to a close, large-scale enterprises became more common, and many businessmen, both competitors and customers, came to believe that the resulting inequality of power was itself a restraint of trade. At the middle of the nineteenth century or perhaps somewhat earlier, the American economy, although characterized by many little local and regional monopolies, was probably as competitive as it has ever been.

During its infancy, even the railroad was deemed as amenable to competition as any other form of economic enterprise. This view persisted until experience showed that competition could not be expected to perform its customary function by providing customers with a satisfactory product or service at a minimum price, through self-regulation by the market.

Contrary to the prevailing ideology, which stressed the beneficence of competition, pooling came to be the accustomed way in which the railroads conducted their business. Although pooling contracts were contrary to the traditional common law, which opposed conspiracies or combinations in restraint of trade, and the Interstate Commerce law of 1887 specifically prohibited pooling, pools proliferated both before and after 1887. The statutory prohibition against pooling was upheld in the Trans-Missouri Freight Association case in 1897, when the Supreme Court invoked the Sherman Antitrust Act.

Those who advocated railroad pooling argued that it was a proper remedy for railroad freight rate discrimination.[33] Its opponents rebutted that pooling was ineffective in curtailing railroad rate discrimination since railroads would continue to strive for a larger allotment at the next division, that pooling destroyed the freedom of the shipper to select which line to use, and that pooling raised the general average of rates.

Pooling adversely affected the interests of large shippers who used competition among railroads to their advantage.[34] In 1886, large shippers testified against railroad pooling before the Cullom committee, a congressional committee that studied interstate commerce and whose efforts resulted in the Interstate Commerce Act. One large shipper, Charles A. Pillsbury, was quite frank: "We think we are getting fully as low freights as the railroads can afford to take the goods for, if not lower."[35]

The greatest interest, and probably the strongest force, in mobilizing opinion was the relation between pooling and the absolute rate level. It was for this reason that Albert Fink testified before the Cullom committee: "The object of the pooling agreements is to enforce the agreed and published tariffs. They have nothing to do with the making of tariffs."[36] Nonetheless, Judson C. Clements, a member of the Interstate Commerce Commission, told the Industrial Commission: "I am afraid that it [making pooling legal] would aggravate the cause of complaint as to excessive rates." To allay such fears George R. Blanchard, a noted railroad expert with a wide range of experience both as operating and pool manager, focused on the rates and not on pooling. He stated: "It is only when pools are used as the means to sustain excessive rates that they are objectionable, and then, as always, the remedy lies in the correction of rates, and not the prohibition of pooling itself."[37] In but a score of years public policy came to agree with this prophet. And by the close of this period, many reformers who had earlier opposed pooling were in favor of it.[38] Impartial students of transportation, shippers, and railroad officials recognized the desirability of pooling, because the large shippers were able to ship their high volume at the lowest rates under the prevailing system, competition among railroads did not work, and discrimination flourished. It was generally conceded that the Interstate Commerce Commission had to have supervision of rates.[39]

Many railroad executives viewed pooling as a legitimate means of restraining competition. One advocated that pooling be made legitimate and placed under governmental supervision:

The strong lines, as a rule, so far as my observations of the matter have gone, are anxious to make the Interstate Commerce Act effectual, but the trouble is with the weaker lines. . . . If a joint arrangement ordinarily known as a "pool" could be operative under the Inter-state Commerce

Act, I believe it would solve many of the difficulties. . . . A railroad once
constructed is built to stay. It must have business to pay the expenses and
fixed charges, and the system of the differential rates has proven an utter
failure. The English roads have been all through this whole matter, and
there through their clearing house, these pools are operative and are I
understand legalized.[40]

And another argued: "I think you will have no difficulty . . . in
convincing the commissioners that the public interest is really
served by the pooling system."

Railroad men thus believed that "maintenance of rates was
'moral,' and surreptitious price competition . . . 'essentially
dishonest.'"[41] One reason was that price reductions dragged the
strong down with the weak! "The force of competition is one that
no carrying corporation can withstand and before which the
managing officers of such a corporation are helpless."[42]

The evidence is strong that railroad leaders considered the difficulties inherent in pooling to be great and that therefore "a
mutual interest in keeping them is the best guarantee that corporations will not break their contracts."[43] Similarly, "sly arrangements
for stealing business, by cutting rates, are sure to be found out
sooner or later, and *when* found out defeat their own object,
besides being at all times, whether found out or not, essentially
dishonest."[44]

Those who tried to cut rates left little record for their defense.
One known incident is of particular interest because the defense
was so bold. The Union Pacific–Northwestern preferential traffic
agreement in October 1889 was protested by Jay Gould on behalf
of the Missouri Pacific, charging that it violated the Interstate
Commerce Railway Association agreement. The Northwestern
admitted the validity of the protest and "stated explicitly that the
traffic contract had been made in defiance of the spirit and even of
the letter of the compact."[45]

Price agreements and pools and other forms of combination
in industry were so common as to constitute the rule rather than
the exception in this epoch, and contemporaries were aware of
this.[46] The motivation was plain enough to the participants: "an
effort is being made to bring about a legal consolidation of the
Carpet Company and firms in New England and elsewhere, for

the purpose of making the investment in the same more profitable than at present."[46]

The cordage industry tried a variety of pools. A cordage pool was dissolved in 1887 because shipments were made in excess of quotas. The National Cordage Company (cordage trust), organized in 1887, tried to corner the raw material market as well as control the supply of cordage machinery. At its peak this firm had 90 percent of the output of the industry, but the Plymouth Cordage Company remained independent and the trust came to an end in 1893.[48]

Such loose agreements were notoriously unstable, because they were not legally enforceable and were contrary to public notions of equity. The Standard Rope and Twine Company (successor to the cordage trust) encountered the same sort of difficulty. An executive acknowledged to the Industrial Commission that "we do have a sort of gentlemen's agreement on prices whereby everybody is bound to live up to the prices, but they do as they please when it comes to the test."[49] This pattern was repeated in industry after industry and was responsible for other forms of consolidation to achieve the same goals with greater effectiveness.

While some criticized pools, especially those who felt themselves threatened, others defended them because of changes in the economy. Charles Elliott Perkins incisively commented to a subordinate:

The tendency of concentration in trade is one which is directly in the interest of greater economy, that is to say the concentration of the oil trade in the hands of the Standard Oil Company cheapens oil to millions of customers, and yet it enables those who control the Standard Oil Company to make themselves rich out of a very small margin of profit. Philosophers may say that it would be better for mankind generally to have the oil business trade managed by four or five hundred concerns, in place of the Standard Oil Company, although it would make consumers pay more for oil than they do now. . . . We do not know whether it would be better or not. Concentration in trade is simply following a law of nature. It is going on everywhere, and if it is against the best interests of society, then it ought to be stopped everywhere, but I do not believe it is against society's interest. Marshall Field makes himself rich selling dry goods by driving other people out of the trade because he sells cheaper than they can afford to. This may send a few hundred dry goods traders to sawing wood or raising corn, but it benefits thousands of consumers.[50]

And Henry Havemeyer of American Sugar Refining in his testimony before the Industrial Commission said:

We maintain that when we reduced the cost we were entitled to the profit, and that it was none of the public's business; we took it and paid it out to our stockholders; it may be business policy to share that with the public sometimes; we did not do it then; we have done it since. We had to increase the output; we could injure our competition by reducing our margin. This is business policy again, not philanthropy. . . . I think it fair to get out of the consumer all you can consistent with the business proposition.

James H. Post, a commission merchant in sugar and agent for independent sugar refiners, defended Havemeyer's firm: "I think that the American Sugar Refining Company has not used the power that it might have used to maintain exorbitant profits. I think it has kept the margin of profit where it paid well for the money invested, but has not sought large profits over that." Still, Post was concerned, as were so many other witnesses before the commission, about the existence of unrestrained power: "Perfect control of any article of universal consumption is a very dangerous thing for any company or any body of men to have. We are all human, and we would naturally use the power it gave us. We would be restricted only by fear of competition."[51]

The fundamental weakness of industrial pools (and hence their replacement by other forms of business organization) was that the firms retained their independent existence and that, if the stakes were high enough, there was great temptation for a member of a pool to seek to expand its market at the expense of its competitors by charging a low price in order to obtain an order. Since pools had no legal standing, other means of enforcement were substituted, and these had their flaws as was revealed by a corporation lawyer in 1902. He testified before the Industrial Commission that it was the large order that broke a pool, because even if a manufacturer has to pay a fine to the pool, he was in a better competitive position. Most important was his comment on the morality of this action: "He [the manufacturer] does not regard it as dishonorable, if it is a 'fine' pool, to pay the $5,000 fine, and then say to his competitors, 'I have paid my fine.' "[52] Exactly what was honorable and what was not is important since in this case a man could act purely pragmatically, unencumbered by any extraneous thoughts on morality. Such a man acted not on the basis of presumed right or wrong but rather on the basis of expediency determined by the presumed economic consequences and the pursuit of strictly business self-interest. If the ends were moral, then all means appropriate to the achievement of these ends were valid.

The impulse for change in business morality concerning restraint of trade came from without. The law, state as well as federal, proclaimed the universalistic standard. Railroad pooling was declared illegal by the Interstate Commerce Act of 1887 as a consequence of clamor from various quarters, but the prohibition hardly can be said to have had a decisive effect. Businessmen, insiders and outsiders, simply could not agree on the morality of such a prohibition. According to Joseph A. Schumpeter, a noted economist, "It makes a great deal of difference whether a given pattern of behavior is condemned by the conscience of the community or supported by a large and vociferous sector of public opinion."[53] Some businessmen actually contended (and it is perhaps fair to note that history a generation later sustained their contention) that pooling was morally defensible because it would tend to diminish rate discrimination, which was also being roundly condemned at the same time. The Sherman Act of 1890 applied to the entire economy and is the most famous expression of the public conscience concerning restraint of trade. But so feeble was the enforcement of the act and so ambiguous was its meaning for more than a decade after its passage that not until the Northern Securities case in 1904, by dissolving a consolidation of several major railroads, was any judicial decision rendered under that law that would cause businessmen to comply with the law. (The railroads constituted an exception to this generalization since the Trans-Missouri and Joint Traffic decisions, in 1897 and 1898, respectively, were strict applications of the Sherman Act.) Still, even the existence of such legislation supplementing the common law could not be ignored indefinitely, and ultimately such impulses for change in business morality pertaining to restraint of trade were augmented by the legal prohibition of specific competitive practices.

COMPETITIVE TACTICS

Businessmen have always used an assortment of competitive tactics in order to stimulate sales and profits, most of them adapted to the market structure and morally sanctioned. The market structure of the earlier world, which featured many buyers and many sellers, enterprises of localized power (though their power might be great within that locality), and an equality of power among enterprises, yielded to one that was almost diametrically opposite.

This new market structure, significant first for railroads by the middle of the nineteenth century and only later for manufacturing, dictated the corruption of the forms of competition. Ever since this structure appeared, ambivalence and divergence of opinion on the morality of the competitive tactics in vogue have characterized the business scene and led to wide discussion.

Competitive tactics in this context refers to those business practices used with maximum impact by large-scale enterprises customarily operating at less than capacity and in industries in which there was imperfect competition. There are three categories of competition: price, product, and promotion. None of these, in and of itself, was immoral or ever so regarded by typical contemporary businessmen or by other than a statistically insignificant minority of Americans. Even price discrimination, the corruption of price competition, was perceived as immoral only in those industries that many contended affected the public interest.

Price discrimination by the railroads continued unabated throughout this period. Although the Interstate Commerce Act was supposed to end discrimination among persons, it did not succeed in doing so. Rate wars alternated with rate stability until the turn of the century.[54] There was less discrimination in times of prosperity than in depression. Railroads were running close to capacity so they had no need to cut rates in order to attract volume. Those who did use price discrimination employed sophisticated methods, such as billing at a lower classification, false weighing, allowances for car mileage, and false billing to a nearer point or a through point. Such methods were used, in connivance with the railroad, by shippers in order to obtain a competitive advantage. Not content with this, some shippers obtained an advantage at the expense of both their competitors and the railroads by false classification, a practice comparable to smuggling.[55]

Generally, railroad executives, shippers, and public officials were antagonistic to rate discrimination as to persons. George Blanchard, former commissioner of the Joint Traffic Association, testified extensively during the hearings of the Industrial Commission. He condemned freight discrimination among persons because "they uniformly upbuild the recipients thereof and as uniformly injure those who do not receive them. They are vicious, indefensible, and illegal in their conceptions and results, whether their results touch one or all of the producers, middlemen, or consumers affected, yet they are most difficult of regulation or stoppage." This last point was seconded by E. P. Ripley (Santa Fe), who declared:

The fact is that the commercial world does not accept the "equal rate" theory. It is just what the railroads want, but what the large shipper does not want. He will theorize that equal rates are best for all, but in his heart and in his practice he believes himself entitled to lower rates than his neighbors of less capital or enterprise. Believing this, he is actively engaged in finding ways to evade the law, and it would be surprising indeed if he fails to succeed.[56]

The mentality of both railroad leader and shipper in accepting discrimination prior to the passage of the Interstate Commerce Act in 1887 is illustrated by the following letters:

Let me suggest that hereafter in similar cases, where the obtaining of a large contract depends upon a slight reduction of the rate of freight, before giving up the matter entirely it might be well for you and I to sit down and discuss the matter. Your interests as a manufacturer and ours as a carrier are mutual, and my experience is that when this is the case, concessions on both sides are finally made which bring out the desired results.[57]

I have just read your letter of March 9, respecting freighting Mr. Cole's brick. I abhor rebates, but at the same time, sympathize with you, and desire to help Mr. C who has been, as I well know, a friend of ours in times past. I think we had better, notwithstanding my horror of rebates, bill at the usual rate, and rebate to Mr. Cole 25 cents a thousand.[58]

Yet others held contrary views about rate discrimination. One railroad president protested to a subordinate that the latter had granted a rebate in violation of a company agreement with competitors.[59] Another railroad officer informed a shipper: "Our rule is that rates of freight should be uniform to all shippers."[60] Rate discrimination, prior to the acceptance by the representatives of the public of a new concept of morality, arose out of the competitive pressure, which tended to depress business morality. Therefore, only a counterpressure in the form of an agreement, implicit or explicit, among competitors could sustain the business morality of the equal rate principle. In the absence of such agreements, competitive pressure strained the business morality of those who wished to adhere to such rules.

It is hardly surprising, therefore, that James C. Clarke, president of the Illinois Central, complained to an official of another railroad about those of his competitors who accepted traffic at less than cost: "My impression is the ills we suffer in R. R. operation are in great degree the fault of management, the want of integrity, candor and fair dealing."[61] In short, there was no unanimity of either action or attitude before 1887 among railroad executives.

Shippers, too, saw the open rates of the railroads as no more than asking prices, although the awareness of both parties that an impropriety existed is evident in the use of oral agreements by men who customarily committed business matters to writing. A Standard Oil executive characterized the pre-1887 world from the vantage point of a large shipper: "It was a man's business to get as low rates as he could." Still, S. C. T. Dodd, who became the Standard attorney in 1879, recognized the existence of and was opposed to what he called "unjust" railroad rate discrimination.[62] Many shippers, especially large ones, assumed that the universalistic ethic justified their seeking preferential treatment from a railroad as from any other purveyor.

It is hardly necessary to offer further proof that railroad freight rate discrimination did not end in 1887. Excess capacity persisted, the sanction of shame was ineffective within the business community, and the sanction of legally determined guilt was all but nonexistent. Although the Interstate Commerce Act was a constraint (even without adequate enforcement), no law could be enforced unless a substantial body of those affected internalized the demands of the law, even if only because it was economically advantegeous to do so. The reduction of excess capacity during the early 1900s, which resulted from prosperous economic conditions and the merger movement in railroads, eased the moral burden on railroad managers. George Blanchard remarked that if a railway man used unfair competitive means, he was rewarded by increased patronage, whereas in other areas he was denounced and debarred from further competition.[63]

At the turn of the century the Industrial Commission explored the matter of railroad freight rate discrimination at length, and the testimony contains argument and counterargument. Discrimination did not find its champions; instead, there were those who explained its origin and continued existence, those who called it morally undesirable but seemingly inevitable, and those who condemned it outright.

Railroads practicing discrimination tended to destroy the evidence of their actions. The testimony of the traffic manager of the Michigan Central before the Interstate Commerce Commission in 1902 constitutes an admission that the man who uses secrecy knows that he is violating the law. Similarly, the traffic manager for the western division of the Pennsylvania admitted that he "destroyed the evidence of the illegal transactions."[64]

William Taussig, a railroad manager, held that large shippers were as responsible as were carriers for rate discrimination.[65] It takes two to strike a bargain, and the crux of the matter was the belief that bargaining was an approved means of establishing a price in a competitive world. "The Southern Pacific sells transportation precisely as a merchant disposes of his wares," one of its executives maintained.[66] Both railroad and shipper, seller and buyer, sought a competitive advantage and defended themselves for doing this. Nevertheless, when asked, "Do you believe that it is morally right?" a railroad man answered in the negative.[67]

The magnitude of the problem more than a decade after the passage of the Interstate Commerce Act is seen in the observation of a corporation lawyer, Charles Claflin Allen:

> It is certainly a safe assertion to make that there is not one large shipper in fifty in any of the great cities of the country, or in any industrial locality, who has not made a large part of his success in placing his goods upon the market through special rates given him by a railroad, or several railroads, lower than the established tariff rate under the law, and therefore in contravention of the law. Yet this act on the part of the shipper, and of the railway company, is by law a crime, and the reputable members of the community who make themselves parties to the unlawful agreement for the discrimination in rates, are either too ignorant, or more often too indifferent, to realize their legal or their moral turpitude.[68]

The position of one of the smaller railroads that probably practiced less discrimination than others was presented by its president. He believed that by obeying the law against discrimination, equilibrium had been established with the shippers, who were satisfied that all received the same treatment and no longer expected the favorable rates that some had received as recently as five years earlier. Significantly, he thought in terms of morality: "We have no right to do it."[69]

One railroad leader who pictured railroad rate discrimination as morally undesirable but seemingly inevitable was Samuel R. Callaway of the New York Central: "They [railroads] are all the same. When one railroad violates the law the other has to." Callaway seemed to be in the grip of competitive forces so beyond his control that he has lost any feeling of individual responsibility.

Melville E. Ingalls, president of the Chesapeake and Ohio, echoed the problem, noting the close relation between morality and the practical consequences of morality:

> This [the decline of discrimination in 1899] has been done by the resolve of the controlling officials that there must be a change, and it has been made much easier by the fact that there was a large amount of business offering, more, in fact, than the capacity of the railways to take care of. A pride has also grown up among managers in obeying the law and discontinuing such practices, and today where here and there a railway manager is supposed to be paying secret rebates he is not looked

upon as in good standing in the fraternity. How long this condition of affairs can last without legislation is a grave question.[70]

Thus the moral resolve and pride of the railroad managers needed the sanction of a larger volume of business so as to reduce the strain of competition and, ultimately, the support of the law.

George Blanchard in his testimony before the Industrial Commission raised an issue of fundamental importance and extended the question of competition to its logical conclusion: "Mr. Carnegie, with all his philanthropies and high character, built a railroad from Pittsburg to Lake Erie to get lower rates than he had enjoyed as a favorite patron."[71]

Large shippers appearing before the Industrial Commission gave widely varied responses to questions on railroad rate discrimination. One conceded that he had been the beneficiary of rate discrimination and that because of it his business had succeeded. Nevertheless he testified: "I do not call that favorable if a man has to violate the law to live [compete] in the land. I stand self-confessed, but I deplore that condition." John D. Archbold of Standard Oil, the most prominent of the shippers examined, stated: "I think we have observed the strict letter of the law [Interstate Commerce Act of 1887] in all that pertains to interstate transportation."[72] Another Standard Oil witness offered an explanation for the company's position:

We might be asked why (in view of the known fact that some of the railroads, since the passage of the interstate commerce law, have paid rebates to large shippers) we have not received same. We have not done so because, in the first place, it was against the law, and secondly, because we knew from past experience that if we received cut railroad rates other oil shippers would receive the same, and we felt, as we now feel, that from a business standpoint alone it has been, and is now, to our interest to have tariff rates maintained.[73]

Morality and profits again marched hand in hand. This point was made by several other witnesses. Archibald S. White, president of the National Salt Company, engaged in the following colloquy:

Q. Do you get lower freight rates than your competitors on account of your very large production?

A. No. We use the published tariff rates.

Q. You use them absolutely?

A. Yes. Strange, isn't it? It is due to the Interstate Commerce law.[74]

And White was echoed by Henry O. Havemeyer, president of American Sugar Refining, who declared: "Under the interstate-commerce act we dare not take a rebate. The Sugar Trust and other trusts are in such odium that they are laying for us fellows so that there would be no escape; there is no advantage in transportation." As a means of coping with the problem of standard rates, the New York railroads and the sugar refiners by agreement allotted each railroad a fixed percentage of the volume of sugar shipped from New York.[75]

The viewpoint of the small shipper was also heard by the Industrial Commission.

The only reason a good merchant seeks a rebate is to put himself on the level of his competitor. He says, "That fellow is getting it; I know he is, and I have to get it if I am going to stay here in business." Now, if he knows that the other fellow is not getting it, the good merchant is not going to waste any time around the railroad office asking for rebates.[76]

Another witness morally equated law as it applied to business with law as it applied to other aspects of life. This man had accepted rebates before 1887 and went out of business in the late 1890s:

I have never taken a rebate since the interstate law went into effect. I did not propose to put myself in the shape of a criminal, and but one man has had the impudence to offer me a rebate since that time. . . . I feel that I have been driven out of business because I would not accept a rebate. . . I did not think that I could do business honestly.[77]

Charles Prouty, a member of the Interstate Commerce Commission, spoke even more to the point: "It is not dishonesty to cut. I do not think the railroads want to cut the rate because they like to be dishonest, but they have to." The commission's final report essentially accepted this conclusion and acknowledged that the cessation of competition would mean the elimination of both the power and the incentive to discriminate since it would protect the virtuous roads from the unscrupulous.[78]

Discrimination as to price was not confined to the railroads, even if the public's attention focused there to the exclusion of its existence elsewhere. Charles J. Harrah, president of the Midvale Steel Company, favored large business combinations because they placed all users or customers on the same basis and tended to charge one price to all. Charles Schwab of Big Steel conceded that some customers paid a freight charge that was greater than usual for the distance the railroad moved the freight. "If you will point out a method of avoiding that we will be very glad," he told his hearers. He believed that "it was perfectly fair . . . to all customers to say what rates of freight would be from specific points."[79] Thus some customers were compelled to pay for freight that moved an imaginary distance although there was no discrimination between customers in the same location. This basing point system of pricing was used in the steel industry, although modified in 1924, until it was abandoned in 1948 as a result of an antitrust decision involving the cement industry.

Price discrimination continued to plague the life insurance field also. The companies paid high commissions to agents, and it was to the mutual advantage of the agent and the customer (as well as the company) for rebates to be granted to the policy holder. One company defended rebating as an example of free trade and said that it could evade the state law prohibiting it.[80] A signed statement by a New York Life agent appeared in a Mutual Life publication: "I am a rebater pure and simple, and not only on business principles but from religious beliefs."[81] Signs of change are evident because the author of this statement was fired by New York Life and expelled from the National Association of Life Underwriters.[82]

Life insurance companies pursued varying policies in regard to rebating, and a few companies eschewed it. In 1893 New York Life prohibited rebating and announced in a circular that its agents who rebated would be fired. This company had a special motive for its action, however; it paid small commissions to agents and would be at a competitive disadvantage in any rebate war.[83] Two years later Northwestern Mutual dismissed several agents who, it had reason to believe, rebated. Its attitude toward rebating was essentially pragmatic; in the long run the practice was bad business.[84] A purchaser of life insurance might resent it if he knew that his skill as a bargainer determined the price he paid and might turn to one of the numerous other companies.

The life insurance industry started with the emphasis on persuading customers to buy a policy from a particular company. This marketing function became uppermost in the 1870s, and during the closing decades of the century, the field shifted to the hands of marketing men.

The drive to the top fostered rebating in order to build volume. The intense competition of the late nineties among the big three— Mutual Life, New York Life, and Equitable Life—encouraged such malpractices by the industry. Complaints were rampant in the insurance press. No single company, it was asserted, could maintain its competitive position if its agents did not grant rebates.[85] In life insurance, although product and promotion competition were present, price competition was frequently decisive.

As the nineteenth century drew to a close, the market for a wide range of products began to be saturated and was less willing to accept whatever was offered by sellers. Also, product differentiation for certain consumer products became possible. In short, promotion competition came to the fore, and manufacturers of consumer products began to use a variety of methods in order to push their products. Some industrial firms used exclusive contracts with dealers in marketing their product. Eastman Kodak was one. It used the strong demand for some of its products as a wedge to sell others that faced more vigorous competition. One of its methods was full line forcing: requiring its dealers to sell only its products if the dealers wished to sell any of them. The counsel of Eastman Kodak supported the inclusion of its policies as part of the universalistic ethic and argued: "I understand in other lines it is common, and the courts have said it is lawful." American Tobacco pursued a similar policy, which obviously served as a barrier to competition. James B. Duke defended it by citing a court ruling that the practice was not a violation of the Sherman Act. Another means to a somewhat similar end was a form of resale price maintenance, in which manufacturers protected their dealers against competition by rewarding those who sold above cost.[86] Such a practice would naturally strengthen the dealer organization and is comparable to the retail price maintenance of more recent years. These, and similar competitive tactics, were effective means of promotion competition in any industry characterized by competition among the few.

For most firms, the competitive tactics and the reasons justifying them did not change until after the turn of the century when business came under the much closer scrutiny of the public. Until then promotion competition, almost unrestrained, continued to motivate consumers. A mass marketer, the Sears, Roebuck Company, sold all manner of products, using advertising to push them and to induce the public to become customers of the great mail order house.

A Sears executive in retrospect justified the advertisement and sale in 1898 of a worthless medical device by reasoning: "Other firms sold it. There was no law against it." Certainly both statements were true; whether the universalistic ethic constituted a wholly adequate defense is another matter. An examination of the publications in which Sears advertised reveals that in the 1890s he was not on a lower ethical plane than his competitors.[87] Richard D. Sears was remembered by a subordinate as having justified a deceptive advertisement on the grounds that it generated inquiries and sold the product.[88] The judgment of the historians of this firm (whose experience was no doubt duplicated by others) is that

the whole story of the quality level of Sears, Roebuck merchandise, of the company business ethics, of the degree of honesty represented in all of its advertising, of the slow development from schemes and sharp practices to a mature philosophy of rigorously honest business—all this story is shot through with contradictions, with backing and filling, with crosscurrents, with inconsistencies.[89]

A method of promotion competition is the adulteration of products either to reduce the cost of production or to make them more marketable. Henry O. Havemeyer of American Sugar Refining testified before the Industrial Commission in favor of government regulation against adulterated food a few years before the enactment of such legislation on the ground that competition could not control that competitive tactic: "There is no way that the consumer can be protected against adulterated food except by law," he asserted.[90] Thus the ability of a seller to deceive the buyer was not seen as making such a practice morally acceptable.

There were a few recorded breaches in the defense of caveat emptor, the implicit and universalistic explanation of promotion competition. Northwestern Mutual Life in the mid-eighties stopped an agent from using overly optimistic advertising in New York newspapers.[91] Another break came in the patent medicine field. During the nineties the N. W. Ayer advertising agency, one of the industry leaders, was critical of the advertising of patent medicines, an important segment of all advertising. Ayer selectively weeded out those advertisers who were the worst.[92] In 1892 the *Ladies' Home Journal* ceased printing patent medicine advertising, and in the following years many newspapers and magazines either refused all medical advertising or attempted to screen out the most objectionable.[93]

Attitudes toward the stealing of industrial secrets by men who would not steal money provide insight into the ambivalent mind of businessmen. Product competition meant either the ability to produce an improved product at a comparable cost or else the ability to produce a comparable product at a reduced cost. Product competition was keen enough so that not only were unpatented products or aspects thereof copied but also patented inventions were frequently copied and counterfeited, and manufacturers treated as public property what legally was not. General Electric defended itself for its industrial espionage on Westinghouse in 1895:

> There is no manufacturing concern in this country that is not more or less interested in the capacity and output of its competitors. The Westinghouse Company has recently completed a factory for which extravagant claims have been made as to capacity and output. . . . Nothing other was done than to verify reports as to capacity and output of the Westinghouse plant as published.[94]

The inference is that General Electric assumed that it had a right to such information. Apparently, in the absence of reliable published information, the firm felt impelled to obtain data in order to compete. The only point at issue was the right method of getting the data.

This incident was apparently rather deliberate; others were much less clear-cut. Around 1900 an employee of the Winchester Repeating Arms Company was assigned by his company to examine certain of the machines of a competitor at its invitation so that he could serve as an expert witness in a trial in which the competitor was one of the parties. As the employee reconstructed it afterward, the following exchange occurred beforehand with Winchester executives.

> *Employee*: There is no objection I suppose to keeping my eyes open and seeing what I can see?
> *President*: Now, Brewer, you are going there at their request, do what they ask you to do, but don't go prying into things that are none of your business.
> *Vice-President*: Why, Tom, there is no objection, is there, to the young man keeping his eyes open.

Apparently Brewer did, for he returned with several new ideas from his sojourn.[95]

The use of secrecy as a competitive tactic transcended all others, since it was a form of business behavior that had universal applicability. In general, businessmen concealed as much as possible from the public, a practice that aroused the suspicion of the public. Silence did not necessarily connote guilt but rather a belief that explanations would not be accepted by others and a feeling that private business was private. A Standard Oil executive opposed supplying data for the House Trust investigation in 1888: "I think this anti Trust fever is a craze which we should meet in a very dignified way and *parry every question* with answers which while perfectly truthful are evasive of *bottom* facts."[96]

Havemeyer told the Industrial Commission that he objected to making the affairs of business public:

There is always an aversion on the part of business men to expose their business to the advantage of competitors, and it is most probable that in case they did give the Government an opportunity to examine their books their condition and their methods would leak out to the injury of themselves and the advantage of competitors.[97]

Charles Claflin Allen, a corporation lawyer, provided a comprehensive explanation of the origin and continued existence of this systematic reticence. He contended that the objection to publicity came from those who began as owner-managers of unincorporated businesses and later became the managers of large-scale, widely-held corporations in which there was a separation of owners and managers: "They have come to think that they have an inherent right to the secrecy and independence to which they are accustomed."[98]

Certainly there is some truth in this observation. Small business has always been less subject to questioning than large, and the men who controlled the industrial giants of 1900 had been schooled in small businesses in an age of what amounted to salutary neglect. Under these circumstances it is not surprising that the process of developing a new morality for managers of large-scale enterprises did not yet include a recognition of the public's right to know. Furthermore, the whole concept of investigation as distinct from legal prosecution, either as a prelude to legislation or for other reasons, was still evolving.

One of the competitive tactics business firms employed was a variant of price competition. It involved matching the prices of competitors in a particular market even if it resulted in price discrimination between markets. The practice was defended as a matter of meeting competition and then, if necessary, raising the price elsewhere to compensate for the reduction. Standard Oil was frequently attacked for this method for the larger adversary certainly had the advantage. During the hearings of the Industrial Commission, John D. Archbold was asked if Standard Oil ever reduced its prices until a rival withdrew from business and then raised its prices. He answered:

We have no such policy. It is possible that, in the zeal and anxiety to serve of some over-zealous servant, such a case might occur. If so, and if it was known, it would not be approved. That is not our policy. We fully realize that if we survive with our business we must treat the public very fairly.[99]

Rather than use secret rebates, W. P. Thompson of Standard Oil told Rockefeller that he advocated the use of open price reductions. He favored "a square fight on open markets" as the "cleanest cut way of doing business." A few years later, another executive suggested to Rockefeller, in advance of his times, that one price should be charged to all.[100] Posted prices open to all did not become common until long after and still do not exist for some commodities. At the turn of the century, men continued to possess mixed views concerning competitive practices. Out of this mixture of dominant and variant value orientations, a new business morality formed with the emphasis on universalism in which all judged according to the same impersonal standard.

Price competition remained by far the most significant form of competition laden with moral overtones. As time went on, railroad rate discrimination as a form of price discrimination was under increasing attack on an ever wider front. The victims, principally smaller shippers, were abetted by some railroad leaders (motivated by a desire to stabilize prices and profits) in efforts to obtain corrective legislation. The railroads proved unable to end discrimination through voluntary cooperation, and the competitive pressure could not be withstood by nondiscriminating railroads.

These railroads, interested in security, seconded the position of most shippers. Values such as these led first to the Interstate Commerce Act of 1887 and then, when that proved to be of limited effectiveness, to a call for more stringent and better enforced legislation. The end of price or rate discrimination enhanced the usefulness of pools and protected ordinary shippers, although it raised gross and net railroad earnings. The equal rate principle as applied to the railroads became part of the universalistic ethic.

Product competition was never of serious social concern. The introduction of new products and the processes used to manufacture them were left to the market. No laws were enacted to inhibit product competition, nor is there evidence of any alteration in business morality in that respect.

Promotion competition was another matter entirely. Some mass media firms declined to deal with socially undesirable products, such as patent medicines, before the law intervened, just as some now refuse to deal with cigarettes. The prevailing view seems to have been that the morality of one's competitors sanctified one's own behavior. Change emanated from the interplay between the internal forces, sometimes pragmatic in origin, and the external.

STOCK WATERING

The concept of the rightness of watered stock varied from industry to industry and within industries. James J. Hill opposed stock watering and was not alone. During the aftermath of the 1893 depression, his railroad (the Great Northern), the New York Central, the Pennsylvania, the Burlington, and the Illinois Central were among those railroads without water in their capitalization. On the other hand, the Erie, the Baltimore & Ohio, the Union Pacific, and the Santa Fe were overcapitalized in the sense that their nominal capitalization exceeded either original or replacement cost.[101] Again, the views of businessmen and others changed; along with the change came either government regulation or the implied threat of it.

Stock watering occurred so often during the late nineteenth century as to seem common practice. It was done by both railroads and industrials, particularly as a by-product of consolidation. The organization of United States Steel was the culmination. The capitalization of this consolidation of consolidations far exceeded the total capitalization of the constituent companies (some of which already contained heavy doses of water), and so the nominal capitalization of Big Steel exceeded the assets.[102]

The basic question concerning watered stock was economic. Some thought that the watering of stock was of no economic significance except to investors and that it had no impact on prices, but others held that the effort to pay dividends on inflated capitalization raised prices. The former view was expressed publicly in 1890 by Charles Francis Adams, Jr.: "I do not think the stock-watering system amounts to much one way or the other."[103] (This is at striking variance with his belief advanced twenty years earlier in "A Chapter of Erie"; in the interim Adams had been both railroad regulator and manager which perhaps accounts for the difference).

The public was suspicious of high profits for railroads, and railroad management recognized this. John Murray Forbes was one: "I rather have a notion that there will not be a chance for more than one stock dividend before bars and barriers are put up, and do not quite like the idea of doing it half way, the one thing is to water and pray which we saints are doing."[104] Other businessmen were aware of public sentiment. An accountant testified before the Industrial Commission that "people always think they are being swindled if a corporation pays more than 6 percent." Yet today stock dividends and splits are routine, because the fiction of par value stock has been removed.

Divergences of opinion were aired before the Industrial Commission between 1898 and 1901. Martin A. Knapp, chairman of the Interstate Commerce Commission, contended that railroad rates were not influenced by capitalization; however, he said: "When it comes to judicial investigation as to what is the proper rate to charge, then comes the question of capitalization and very properly so."[105]

John H. Reagan, chairman of the Railroad Commission of Texas, linked rates, profits, and capitalization more strongly when he declared to the Industrial Commission: "What the [railroad] company is entitled to ask is a fair return on the value of that which it employs for the public convenience." The public had an implicit idea of a fair return and watered stock made the rate of return appear to be lower than it was in actuality. Another public witness, Edward Webster Bemis, spoke to the same point: "They [public utilities] always had a tendency to overcapitalize, because it deceived the public as to their profits . . . they [investors] think there may be a demand by the public for a reduction of charges." One of the outstanding academic experts of his day, William Z. Ripley, concurred: "The question of the reasonableness or unreasonableness of rates rests upon the amount of actual investment there is in that road." This view completely denied the validity of entrepreneurial profits. Agreement was also voiced by Henry C. Adams, statistician of the Interstate Commerce Commission, who noted that the courts had adopted the theory that reasonable rates must have some direct or indirect relation to the valuation of railroad properties (and hence to capitalization).[106]

Businessmen also cited the objection to stock watering in its relation to rates and profits. Paul Morton of the Santa Fe stated quite bluntly: "I don't believe in the watering of stock." An independent corporate accountant, Thomas L. Greene of the Audit Company of New York, rendered his judgment:

> I think it is a great deal better for a road to pay high dividends than it is for it to water its stock. . . . [but] the sentiment of the community is against high dividends. Therefore, in order to cover that, the people who manage these affairs have thought that they are compelled to increase the capitalization so as to make the rate of dividends about the same as before.

E. R. Chapman, a banker and broker, conceded that in the case of a regulated public utility, there was more danger of having the rate reduced if the company was undercapitalized and paid a high percentage dividend than vice versa.[107]

The Industrial Commission concluded that the weight of opinion was against watered stock largely because it tended to sustain rates:

> The chief objection to capitalization on the basis of earning capacity is that it obscures the relation between rates, wages, and profits. It is impossible to discover, without a careful appraisal of the property, whether an overcapitalized road is earning more than a fair return upon the investment. The principle is generally accepted at the present time that capital is not entitled to more than a certain fair rate of profits. The issuance of additional securities on the basis of increasing earning power makes it possible for a company covertly to secure exorbitant returns on the actual investment. This objection seems conclusive against the policy of full capitalization up to the limit of earning power.

The problem lay in the dilemma of two or more railroads, in competition, with different capitalizations and different efficiencies. Theoretically they would be entitled to different rates, but they would, in fact, have to charge identical rates. It further assumed as an act of faith that although capitalization had no direct connection with rates, it did have an indirect one: "In the long run excessive capitalization tends to keep rates high; conservative capitalization tends to make rates low."

High capitalization tends, moreover, to keep up rates by preventing voluntary concessions which might otherwise have taken place. A company paying high dividends may find it expedient to lower its rates in order that exorbitant profits may not excite a hostile public opinion. But if returns from excessive rates can be distributed in dividends on watered capital, the public is not aroused to demand reductions. High capitalization, therefore, has at least an indirect bearing on rates. The amount of railroad capital is not to be regarded as a matter of no concern to shippers.

The essence of the argument was that high rates of profit by public service corporations would result in public demand and regulatory action in the direction of lowered prices more readily than if the same amount of profit was distributed over a greater capitalization.[108] Since competition could not control railroad rates, the earning capacity should not be capitalized.

Watered stock was different in the industrial sector of the economy from what it was in the public utility field, because the former was more competitive. In the latter, the existence of public commissions vested with rate-making authority was a recognition of this. Many businessmen at the close of the century thought that earning power alone (not earning power and physical assets) constituted the proper basis for capitalization of industrial common stocks. According to one view, railroad capitalization for purposes of rate making should be dependent on physical assets. After a prolonged legislative struggle, the Valuation Act of 1913, which established the original or replacement cost of each railroad as the basis for determining rates, epitomized this view. Incidentally, the government's physical valuation program about fifteen years later revealed that the capitalization of the railroads included little if any water and that the physical assets of the railroads were worth what they were purported to be. On the other hand, industrialists thought it ethical to issue stock for more than the book value of the assets since this was regarded as irrelevant, and they believed that in such cases no water was added. This idea was criticized by some financial writers.[109]

Leaders in the iron and steel industry held widely divergent views. One contended to the Industrial Commission that over-capitalization (beyond tangible assets) in the case of large combinations tended to result in an attempt to pay dividends on the capitalization through higher than normal prices. He thus saw a parallel between the imperfect competition in certain industries and the public utilities (natural monopolies). On the other hand, Charles Schwab, president of United States Steel, denied that the claimed overcapitalization of this combination and some of its predecessor companies would have any impact on prices from the point of view of paying dividends on the capitalization. Schwab defended earning power as the proper basis of capitalization.

American Sugar Refining's Havemeyer said that he based capitalization on earning capacity and claimed that a trademark (brand name) could be just as valuable as (or more so than) a physical asset. When asked if it was a fair proposition for the consumer to pay dividends on watered stock, Havemeyer retorted, "I do not care two cents for your ethics. I do not know enough of them to apply them. . . . As a business proposition it is right to get all out of a business that you possibly can. . . . If you get too much of a profit, you get somebody in competition."[110]

The Industrial Commission decided that the American Sugar Refining Company was heavily overcapitalized in terms of physical assets although it paid high dividends: "This raised the question whether the power of the combination has not enabled it to keep prices up so that its earnings could pay dividends on an excessive capitalization, and whether the high capitalization has not been an added temptation to hold prices high."[111] Certainly if this conclusion is accepted, then the supposed differences between regulated public utilities and industry fade away. In both cases there was the same trio of capitalization, prices, and profits. In neither was competition wholly absent, but in neither (if attention is confined in industry to those industries with high concentration ratios and large-scale enterprises) was it absolutely present. Not even perfect monopolies can charge just any price. In any case, a business would try to maximize profits if allowed; any limit to a certain percentage would have to be based on a physical valuation.

Perhaps the alleged differences between the regulated and non-regulated sectors of the economy regarding stock watering were unduly magnified. Jay Gould's hypothesis was that earning power was the proper means of valuing all enterprises.

> I judge all properties myself by their net earning power. . . . You may say there is "water" in the Western Union Company [Gould's current interest]; so there is "water" in all this property along Broadway. This whole island was once bought from the Indians for a few pounds of tobacco, and a few strings of beads, and everything that has been put in since you may say is "water." But no; the value of this property is judged by its earning power. . . . Now that is the way to value a railroad or a telegraph line, and, judged by that rule, the Western Union is worth what it earns— a net income of 7 per cent—on its capital. . . . That would be [over] $100,000,000 . . . [in capital].[112]

The range of opinion concerning the morality of watered stock can be summarized briefly. First, there was a distinction in the minds of many men between the particularistic ethics that pertained respectively to the regulated and the unregulated sectors of the economy. Second, the sentiment of shippers opposing watered stock in the railroads, by far the most important segment within the regulated sector, later crystallized itself in the acceptance, by representatives of the electorate acting through legislatures, of a new universalistic ethic; rates were separated from nominal capitalization and appeals were made to use real capitalization as the basis for rates. Third, many in the industrial sector advocated the use of earning power as the basis for determining the capitalization of an enterprise. In this sector watered stock was not placed beyond the bounds of the universalistic ethic until the so-called Securities Acts of 1933–1934, although in those the prime purpose was the protection of unwary or uninformed investors and not the general public, since stock watering afforded insiders an advantage at the expense of outsiders.

FINANCIAL REPORTING

As the characteristics of the leading enterprises altered, new financial reporting techniques were devised in order to cope with new problems. The traditional ones were inadequate for the purpose of providing adequate financial reporting even for the sole purpose of managerial decision making. Furthermore, the number of communities (outsiders) to whom the owner-managers (insiders) were in some way responsible expanded, and each of these communities had an interest that in some way was separate from, and perhaps antagonistic to, that of the owner-managers.

The beginning of big business in the American economy during the middle decades of the nineteenth century meant that there were men who, as the century drew to a close, could recall a time when business was a private affair and financial reports were prepared only for management. For a long time business letters continued to be penned by the writer and were considered to be for the eyes of the addressee only, without intervention of a secretary (who would be male and possibly ambitious). This was considered not merely good business practice but good etiquette. Secrecy was important. If word of difficulty leaked out, competitors, creditors, and customers might be led to take action adverse to the interest of the firm and its owner-managers. Under such circumstances, it is by no means surprising that the early financial reports submitted to stockholders, regulatory agencies, or the general public were no more readily available or more reliable than those provided by an individual about himself.

Businessmen under such circumstances could shade the truth, exaggerate, misrepresent, or remain silent, because they applied a particularistic ethic intended to protect members of their particular community. Also there was a tendency for management to treat those stockholders who were not part of management as outsiders, if not actually in league with the competition, and apply the appropriate morality. Consequently it becomes easy to comprehend why some businessmen were able, without any qualms whatsoever, to tell the outsider whatever he wanted to hear about an enterprise or whatever suited the interest of the insider. As financial reporting techniques and standards improved, as professionalization appeared both in management and those who served it, and as the efforts of regulatory agencies became more effective, information became more complete and dependable. Consensus as to what was moral was also fostered by more rigorous demands of government and by the need to satisfy the scrutiny of one's creditors and owners. George Stephen, one of James J. Hill's closest associates, writing in 1893 from the London capital market, complained that the Great Northern annual report was insufficiently detailed. Hill denied the allegation but soon furnished his English financial allies with an inside financial report.[113] The universalistic ethic slowly replaced the particularistic ethic as financial reports became more reliable and more accessible, and all men began to be part of the universal order.

Top management supplied investors (and the general public) with minimal financial reports during the closing years of the nineteenth century.[114] Enterprises in the unregulated sector of the economy (for instance, manufacturing) were not obligated to submit financial reports even to such outsiders as stockholders and hence disseminated such limited financial reports as suited management. Much therefore depended on such factors as the size of the enterprise, its legal form, the number of owners, the proportion of shares owned by insiders, and the existence of bonded indebtedness. (Such firms are still able to engage in interpretation to a considerable extent in the preparation of their financial reports.)

The railroads were a regulated industry although the regulations governing financial reports varied considerably from one jurisdiction to another. The profit and loss account was particularly subject to manipulation by railroads. After difficulties lasting a decade, the Baltimore & Ohio was forced to undergo a reorganization precipitated by the depression of 1893. An independent examination in 1896 by an accountant, Stephen Little, revealed that the books of the company erred in various ways so as to inflate earnings by about $11 million.[115] An Erie reorganization committee under Drexel, Morgan & Co. discovered in 1895 that the net earnings of the recent past were based on nonrecurring income.[116] The Wabash paid preferred dividends in 1881, although the net earning did not justify it, but Gould published only gross, not net, earnings. The Wabash under Gould in 1882 and 1883, in order to show net earnings, charged operating expense items to construction.[117] Stephen Little was the expert auditor who revealed in 1894 that the Atchison, Topeka & Santa Fe had manipulated its accounting reports. For four years preceding, this railroad had violated the law by paying rebates, and in order to conceal this practice, and for other reasons, it falsified its books.[118] The Santa Fe during the 1890–1894 period overstated its profits, added the amount paid out in rebates to assets, overstated cash, accounts receivable, and property, and understated bills payable just as other railroads often minimized profits.[119]

The public did not have access to an adequate quantity of reliable financial information. The universalistic ethic, which regarded business as the private affair of the managers, led to ambivalence or strong opposition to revealing details of operation. Charles Elliott Perkins, a railroad leader whose reputation for probity among his peers was unsurpassed, held strikingly inconsistent views. He told his mentor, "The less said in a public report the better."[120] But his advice to an inferior was that "Public opinion which necessarily regulates us all in the long run, is not unreasonable, but it is sometimes without proper information on which to base its judgment."[121] The tariff and income tax proposal of 1894 prompted an outburst by an executive of the Pepperell Manufacturing Company: "I would burn them [the books] rather than submit to such degradation. If the Income Tax bill passes, we can be forced to show everything and for that reason I trust the Tariff bill will never be passed."[122] It was the pending necessity of making his business public, and not the money to be paid, that aroused this man's ire.

In the absence of uniformity based on the existence of enough knowledge, as well as the desire to apply that knowledge, considerable scope was available for the exercise of the businessman's creative impulses. Depreciation remained something of a mystery, even at the very highest levels:

It should be manifestly wrong to sell an engine which was partly worn out in the service and credit the amount received to Equipment, and then charge the cost of a new engine to Equipment account, thus making the Equipment account stand the depreciation instead of Operating account, where it properly belongs.[123]

Discretion was present in the assignment of particular items to the various accounts. The desired result can often explain the motivation for an action. In 1883 Milton H. Smith, an executive of the Louisville & Nashville, criticized its financial reporting in a letter to its president, whom he soon succeeded: "The practice of charging expenditures of one year to the account of the succeeding is reprehensible, and cannot be defended. The assigned reasons are puerile and disingenuous."[124] Conservative financiers regarded the inflation of the construction (capital) account as improper, but even the most ethical railroad executives charged construction expenses to operations in order to reduce taxes.[125] One executive proposed to his president the reduction of the book value of assets subject to taxation.[126] The sheer complexity of the financial structure of some firms led to this exchange before the Industrial Commission:

Q. Then the subsidiary corporations often made it possible to make fictitious returns and earnings.
A. Not exactly fictitious—I do not care to call them fictitious . . . but misleading returns and earnings.[127]

The possibility of manipulation on a colossal scale was still present in this era, as the exceptional case of the Santa Fe indicates. Joseph W. Reinhart was hired by the Santa Fe as an auditor to improve the bookkeeping, and he became president in 1893. He resigned the following year as the man nominally responsible for juggling the accounts.[128] Shortly after his resignation, Reinhart is reported to have complained:

Had I been able to distribute over my suspense account $2,000,000 of rebates the books would have been all right, but there never has been a time when I could distribute all these matters with safety. Of course rebates are pledged by agents without the knowledge of the accounting department and then they come in in lump sums where they don't belong and they have to be distributed.

The reactions of some of the participants to his statement were startling. Benjamin P. Cheney, Jr., active in the express business and as a railroad director and a member of the Santa Fe board for many years, confided:

If he [Reinhart] had had any sporting blood in him he would have called

[Stephen] Little [the auditor who examined the Santa Fe's books] a liar to his face [at the public confrontation of Little and Reinhart in 1894] even if he apologized to him privately. He should have bluffed the whole thing off and held his nerve instead of being taken by astonishment.[129]

Financial reporting improved only during the latter part of this era, in part because of the beginning of the imposition of uniform accounting practices in railroads as required by the Interstate Commerce Act of 1887. Accounting manuals also came into use, although there was more than one on railroad accounting. Although this process was not completed for a generation, the fact that reports took a uniform aspect made deviants highly visible. By the close of the century, Thomas F. Woodlock, railroad editor of the *Wall Street Journal*, was able to claim: "It is pretty much impossible for a railroad to do that [charge as capital assets items that should have been charged as operating expenses] without its being incidentally jumped upon." He noted that the listing requirements of the New York Stock Exchange, still a totally unregulated private club, had improved the publicly available financial reports of the railroads, and probably elsewhere as well: "I cannot call to mind a single important road today that does not make a reasonably good report."

What constituted a reasonably good report then would hardly be the same today, if only because of the passage of so much subsequent legislation. A former railroad executive concurred in Woodlock's general judgment but explained it as the result of the reform that ensued after the depression of 1893.[130] Probably thorough reevaluation of standard operating procedures was instigated by those who suffered as a result of financial reports that failed to tell the truth.

The pressures of the marketplace, as well as those of past practice, contributed to the tendency of financial reporting to remain unchanged. But there were pressures for change emanating from several different quarters. Railroads and other forms of regulated economic activity were required to submit ever more comprehensive financial reports to the commissions responsible, imposing a higher level of competence on management. The competitive process itself had the same effect since the management of a multiproduct, multiplant firm demanded superior knowledge of costs, sales, and profits if the enterprise was to prosper. Lastly, the evolution of middle management stimulated the mobility of managers, and they transferred their skills from the old employer to the new one.

Much more important, these factors fostered a spectrum of behavior within the business community that resulted in the spread of improved financial reporting from the railroads to other sectors of the economy, such as manufacturing, which trailed behind. Railroad management frequently participated in the management of other forms of economic activity—for example, manufacturing. This practice diffused rather widely the financial reporting policies and values of the railroads, a sector of the economy that was compelled to open up earlier and more extensively than most others. Perhaps another reason was a growing sense of responsibility of insiders to outsiders—stockholders, bondholders, investment bankers, regulatory agencies, and the general public—none of whom could be assumed to be passive victims. The conflict of values within a businessman, an enterprise, or an industry was invariably resolved in favor of improved financial reporting as a combination of pressures succeeded in overcoming inertia. By the turn of the century, all of the various interests had access to financial reports that were generally superior to those of one or several generations earlier. Financial reporting was less subject to the arbitrary whim of management at the time of the Industrial Commission than it had been during the Hepburn investigation or when state regulatory agencies first appeared.

Surely entrepreneurs in this era followed patterns of business ethics unlike those of the present, but there is no reason to believe that the heads of large-scale enterprise were less ethical than their predecessors of an earlier generation. The letters Cochran examined "suggest that much of the behavior of railroad executives objected to by contemporary moralists was simply the carrying out on a large scale of the aims and cultural beliefs of American business society."[131] Moreover, the railroads strongly influenced American business society at this time.

The accepted rules did change, and for the better. At the start of the period 1880–1900, the code of business ethics was not clearly defined, and it varied among places, industries, situations, and individuals. Some business men raised the general level of business morality, while others did the reverse, but the drift of change was clear. Again and again, those with a grievance against business because of certain practices and those who felt deceived by some businessmen agitated and called upon government to act. It did, passing the Interstate Commerce Act. Although the resulting Interstate Commerce Commission was impotent during this era to eradicate railroad freight rate discrimination, it nonetheless collected evidence, conducted hearings, rendered judgments, participated in trials, obtained publicity, and challenged businessmen to take a stand on the moral implications in rate making. Slowly the practice held in disrepute was brought under control. Eventually businessmen internalized, however grudgingly, the values of the community, if only to avert conflict with it.

One of the common defenses of unethical behavior was that managers behaved as they did because of orders from a higher authority. Samuel Spencer, president of the Southern Railway at the turn of the century, expressed his opposition to this idea most forcefully to the Industrial Commission:

Now, I do not agree at all in the view it is a hardship upon a subordinate or upon a superior that he shall be required to obey the law even when he is face to face with the crucial point, "Must I obey the law or lose my situation?" The law does not recognize the right of a man to make a living illegally or criminally and I do not see how he should be allowed to do it in the railroad business when he is not in any other. I am willing the penalty should be applied wherever it fits. There may be difficulties in reaching the right man, but the man who is responsible can be reached if sufficient effort is made. if you are the right man, or I am, no distinction should be made, whether it is the president or a subordinate. . . . If I can not choose properly whether I shall become a criminal or go out of business, I do not deserve much sympathy.

Here is a clear public statement that moral choice and responsibility exist in business as elsewhere.

Although businessmen began to constrain their behavior, they realized that lax enforcement of the law allowed deviants competitive advantages. As Spencer testified:

> The fundamental objection to that system [which uses illegal competitive methods] of doing business I think is its illegality. . . . I think fundamentally this whole question of transportation, like everything else, should be based upon a recognition of law as it exists. . . . It [violation of the law] puts the law-abiding citizen at a disadvantage. It has a business aspect as well as a moral one. An injury is being inflicted upon him because of the fact that he obeys the law. . . . It [violation of any law] weakens the moral force of the community at large.

Even more pointed were the remarks of Samuel R. Callaway, president of the New York Central: "I do not think the majority of the people fly in the face of the sentiment of the community for any length of time." John W. Gates (American Steel and Wire) agreed: "I was president of that company, and was president of an association—which was possibly contrary to law—a few years ago that sold the products. We discovered that we were infringing on some of the various trust laws and we discontinued that business."[132]

The influence of public opinion, both as a direct force and as it was exerted through the legislative process, should not be discounted. A corporation lawyer explained that a legal reorganization had occurred because of it:

> Mainly because there have been laws passed by the United States, and a number of States, that were inimical to the [trust] form of organization, and the great public prejudices had been aroused, which seriously affected the values of the shares of the trust, and we had a great desire to conform to all of the laws of the country, and to the views which were taken by the public of that form of organization.

The head of a local railroad put it as simply as possible to the Industrial Commission: "I do not cut rates. There is a law against cutting rates, and I am . . . a law-abiding man, and I don't cut rates."[133]

Some entrepreneurs scored the problem of the effect of a law that was not supported by the people. Melville E. Ingalls, a railroad president at the end of the century, thought that the penal provisions of the Interstate Commerce Act rendered it ineffective:

> When you provide a punishment for an act committed by an officer of a corporation in the way of business which is done every day by 90 per cent of the businessmen engaged in private affairs without punishment, you are making that a crime which the public conscience does not consider one, and therefore such a law has not the support of the public. The public will not support anyone, either a railway official or a businessman, who gives information leading to conviction under such a law. . . .

> A man selling goods is on the same basis as the railway man selling transportation. The public does not consider it a crime to sell the goods at a lower price to one than another. You have not educated your communities outside of the railways to the view that discrimination in selling transportation is a crime; therefore, when you hope to pass beyond what public opinion thinks is justified you do not succeed.

Others doubted the effectiveness of the law. John E. Cowen, president of the Baltimore & Ohio Railroad, was one:

> I think we have got to follow the scriptural rule, "The Kingdom of heaven is within you." There must be something from within, because we must curtail it ourselves.
> My question is, to use the same rule, when the Kingdom of heaven is within the railroad managers would not a little help from the outside make it more general.
> It might.

But George Blanchard, long a railroad executive, thought differently: "Railway officers and patrons can not be legislated into mutual rectitude when otherwise disposed, for even the Divine Laws have not done that. They must be afforded some positive aids to betterment."[134]

Publicity was seen as improving business behavior, just as bright street lighting is a deterrent to crime. Charles A. Prouty, a member of the Interstate Commerce Commission, believed that the inspection of the books of the railroads, even the possibility that they might be inspected, would decrease discrimination.

The most compelling denial of law as a constraint on business behavior came in the testimony of an executive of the Southern Pacific. According to him, the constitution of California empowered the state to declare rates, and the California Railroad Commission approved all tariffs, but he conceded to the Industrial Commission: "I do not think that the Southern Pacific as a company would be willing to recognize, notwithstanding the constitution, that it [the California Railroad Commission] had the power the constitution pretends to give it; but still the commission has from time to time caused considerable reductions in tariffs."[135] In this era of weak government and strong business, the latter thought itself entitled to contend with the former on equal terms.

Although it is true that at this time the word *soulless* usually preceded *corporation*, not everyone accepted this view. Charles Claflin Allen, a corporation lawyer, stated that *corporation* implied an element of individual intent: "There is in the idea always the suggestion of a moral factor, a living being, capable of thinking, and feeling, and acting upon his thoughts and feelings." Of course, not everyone agreed. Stuyvesant Fish, a railroad executive, argued that a corporation had no morality.[136] And Henry Havemeyer denied the validity of the separation between the corporation and the individual: "There appears to be in the public mind a distinction between robbery by an individual and that by a corporation. What is commendable in an individual appears to be dishonest in a corporation. I maintain that it is immaterial to the public in what form business is done—whether by an individual, firm, corporation or even trust."[137]

By the late nineteenth century, businessmen, pressured by external criticism, had come to judge each other by more than industry standards. Occasionally the particularistic dominated the universalistic, illustrated by Charles T. Yerkes, the Chicago traction magnate, who stood condemned by those who knew him best. One was quite harsh: "I believe he would stop at nothing. He would dare any means to carry a point that seemed to him essential."[138] Peter A. B. Widener and William L. Elkins, Yerkes's associates who ultimately bought him out, more than once complained that Yerkes "double-crossed his best friends in all his deals."[139] Yet businessmen regarded the breach of trust within the club as a much more heinous offense than any such act inflicted on outsiders.

Still some believed that businessmen could not be trusted. At a general railroad conference called by J. P. Morgan and attended by representatives of sixteen western railroads, A. B. Stickney of the Chicago, St. Louis & Kansas City Railroad was reported to have commented: "I have the utmost respect for you, gentlemen, individually, but as railroad presidents, I wouldn't trust you with my watch out of my sight."[140]

In 1898 William Taussig, ex-president of the Terminal Railroad Association of St. Louis, spoke before a businessmen's club. His topic, "The Ethics of Railway Management," was subsequently printed by order of the club. In his speech he expounded a point of view with which his colleagues no doubt were familiar and to which they were willing to listen. Taussig maintained that each railway officer had his own code established with or without reference to his own conscience: "The individual conscience of a railway officer is a distinct and separate moral quality from his official conscience. Many an officer would, under no circumstances, consent to do in private life what his official conscience permits him to do in the discharge of his official duties." "In between the personal and official conscience of many railway officers," he noted, "many cases may arise in which a strict interpretation of some of the Ten Commandments would lead to some perplexities." Illegitimate business methods, he observed, were commonly defended on the grounds that business is analogous to war and that the end justifies the means. But Taussig objected to this reasoning. The soldier was required to surrender his individuality and consequently neither civil nor moral law held him responsible. But this was not true of those who work for railroads. Moreover, because a businessman's actions affect the public, there is an ethical side to what appeared to be business matters.[141]

The private comments of two railroad executives substantiate Taussig's thesis that there was no recognized code for the railways: "There is no sentiment in business. When a proposition of the character submitted [profit potential complicated by moral implications] is offered to an Executive Committee, it is usually promptly accepted without much reference to any feature beyond the mere gain involved."[142]

This dichotomy between business activity and ordinary moral behavior may help to account for Henry Villard's resolution of the tension between ends and means: "In my long and varied railroad experience I happen to have learned that a little boldness and temporary disregard of mere forms often prevents disastrous results."[143]

It is clear that by the end of the nineteenth century, business morality was upgraded. Men thought and behaved differently than they had twenty years earlier. The universalistic ethic expanded, while the particularistic ethic shrank.

4

THE AGE OF CONFIDENCE 1900 ~ 1914

The new century opened with the land frontier closed according to the Census Bureau, but the frontier of economic opportunity remained open. Problems of evolving business morality persisted, although by 1914, the standards increasingly approached those commonly held today.

A variety of factors continued to exert a force for change in the early 1900s. External pressures were particularly strong for managers of large-scale enterprises, for several reasons. First, much criticism appeared in both newspapers and periodicals. Second, additional restraining legislation provided new and more specific rules. Last, hearings on pending legislation added new facts, helping to stimulate and crystallize opinion. And other factors—university schools of business were getting underway and managers were becoming increasingly professionalized—had some limited effect. In short, the process by which the universalistic ethic displaced the particularistic continued.

CONFLICT OF INTEREST

By the opening of the twentieth century, railroad construction was rarely done through an inside construction company. Among the numerous reasons were a decline of new construction, increased publicity and regulation, greater financial strength of the individual roads, population and freight generally present in advance of railroad construction, and, finally, changes in the moral code. One exception, which occurred in 1897, was not uncovered until 1913, when the road went bankrupt. Benjamin F. Yoakum, chairman of the board of the St. Louis and San Francisco (Frisco) Railway, had participated in the construction of certain subsidiary lines that were sold to the parent company.[1]

Conflict of interest took a somewhat different form with Stuyvesant Fish, president of the Illinois Central. Fish deposited Illinois Central funds in a weak bank, of which he was a director, and loaned Illinois Central money to himself on poor collateral.[2] E. H. Harriman, the dominant shareholder, ousted Fish as president in 1906 because of this conflict of interest, writing to a fellow director of the Illinois Central, "It [this episode] indicated that he [Fish] looked upon the Illinois Central as his personal property to be used as he personally saw fit."[3] In that same year the railroad adopted a new bylaw: "Except upon the precedent vote of the Board of Directors, none of the funds or securities of the company shall be directly or indirectly loaned to any director or officer of the company, nor to any firm of which he is a partner."[4] The possibility of a future impropriety was thus removed as part of the aftermath of a dispute between insiders.

Insiders inherently possessed access to valuable information before releasing it to the public as is illustrated by the following episode. Edward H. Harriman withheld the news of a dividend increase from the public for two days after the directors of the Union Pacific met. The speculative potential for the insiders was considerable. There is, however, no evidence that Harriman and the board members exploited this opportunity. Harriman defended himself for the delay on the grounds that two directors had been absent from the meeting.[5] Presumably he thought that all the insiders should be afforded a chance to learn of this decision before any outsiders.

Conflict of interest remained endemic in large-scale enterprises and had to be combatted. After Judge Elbert H. Gary became chairman of the newly formed United States Steel Corporation, advantages to insiders through conflict of interest situations decreased.[6] "In the Steel Corporation," Charles M. Schwab, its first president, reminisced years later, "I had to fight the directors all the time until one day I said at the Board meeting, 'I believe I am the only man on this board who has not something to sell to the Steel Corporation.'[7] Equally, Standard Oil was concerned with protecting itself, as evidenced by management's words to a subordinate: "I [Daniel O'Day in 1903] write for the purpose of saying that it is contrary to the policy of the Company to allow any of its employees to become interested in the producing business, as it leads to many things."[8]

Conflict of interest within the financial community took several forms. The investment banker was both the seller of securities and, as officer and director of banks and life insurance companies, the buyer. Bank officers and directors also borrowed from their own banks, and officers and directors of banks and insurance companies were personal participants in security flotations in which their companies were also interested. Of these, the interrelations between the insurance companies as buyers and the investment bankers as sellers received the most searching exposure.[9]

Washington Life was acquired by Thomas Fortune Ryan, who transferred its investments from real estate and mortgages to securities bought through his brokerage houses and companies in which he was interested.[10] All of the Big Three (Equitable, Mutual, and New York) life insurance companies invested heavily in securities.[11] (Of these, the last, New York, whose executive vice-president, George W. Perkins, was both chairman of the finance committee and a partner in J. P. Morgan and Company, had by far the highest percentage of its assets in securities.) Their officers were thus participants in security syndicates in which their companies participated.[12] As measured by the rate of return, these companies had a poor investment record in comparison with other similar companies.[13] Prudential was the only one of the largest insurance companies that, at the time of the Armstrong inquiry, did not participate in investment syndicates and then only because it had been required by a court decision in 1903 to buy only on the open market.[14]

The Armstrong insurance investigation, conducted by a New York legislative committee from 1905 to 1906, emanated from the public exposure of an internal contest for control within the Equitable Life Assurance Society of the United States. *Commercial and Financial Chronicle*, a highly influential weekly, commented tartly that there was "so much that is unsavory, so much that offends the moral sense" in the Equitable situation.[15] The record of this investigation reveals details of such conflict-of-interest situations. Favored insiders, for example, were able to make collateral loans at very favorable interest rates, and New York and Metropolitan exchanged such favors to their insiders on a reciprocal basis.[16] Mutual, another large firm, became an owner of the Guaranty Trust Company, and some of its trustees were also on the board of directors of the bank. It used the bank both as an investment and as a place for deposits. Mutual trustees were also on the directorates of other concerns, and its investment portfolio reflected this.[17] Equitable controlled the Mercantile Trust Company, had large interests in two others, and maintained large cash balances. The large and continuous cash flow of the insurance companies was used by the officers to further their individual interests.[18] The result of this complex of conflicts of interest was that insiders benefited at the expense of the insurance companies and the policy holders, because the rate of return on the investments was reduced.

Louis D. Brandeis was one of the sharpest critics of the role of the investment banker. He objected to investment bankers serving as both buyers and sellers and charged that "no man can serve two masters."[19] Jacob Schiff, of Kuhn, Loeb & Company, was also a director of Equitable Life and sold securities to the latter despite the existence of a law prohibiting any life insurance director from profiting in or aiding in the sale of securities.[20] When J. P. Morgan invited George W. Perkins to become a member of J. P. Morgan and Company, Morgan wanted Perkins to leave New York Life because of the conflict of interest.[21] But Perkins declined to resign from the insurance company, and Morgan accepted him as a partner on those terms in 1900. In 1902 Perkins suggested to the New York Life finance committee that the deposit account with J. P. Morgan and Company be closed, but the committee refused to do so.[22]

William W. Armstrong, chairman of the committee bearing his name, questioned Perkins:

When in your judgment, are you acting for the New York Life?
All the time.

When are you acting for J. P. Morgan and Company?
It depends on what the actual case is. Mr. Chaiman . . .
I know when a transaction comes to me . . . I take up that question
and dispose of it as I see my duty.

Charles Evans Hughes, counsel of the Armstrong committee, queried Perkins about a transaction in which the seller was J. P. Morgan and Company and the buyer was New York Life; Perkins represented both parties and claimed to have obtained a "bargain" in one transaction. When Hughes asked, "Did you bargain for them with any person other than yourself?" Perkins replied, "I think I did it myself, probably."[23]

Perkins was also involved in another conflict of interest: he did not separate the Nylic investment fund for the agency directors of New York Life from his personal investments. Hughes again questioned Perkins:

Don't you keep a separate fund for the Nylic money?
No, sir, I do not.
How do you discriminate between your individual interests and your
duty as trustee?
I do as my judgment dictates in each instance. . . .
You do not regard yourself as liable to an accounting?
I do not . . . but I would certainly regard myself as morally responsible
if I made any substantial loss.
Morally, but not legally?
Not morally, but I would make it good.[24]

Perkins did not personally profit in this instance (and Nylic's investments were profitable), but he might have abused his trust, and no one would have known.

The Armstrong investigation in New York was followed immediately by a similar one in Wisconsin in 1906. The three firms (Northwestern Mutual, Wisconsin, and Union Life) that Wisconsin examined emerged relatively well with regard to financial practices. The committee uncovered no conflict of interest in security purchases, no syndicate participations by officers, and no use of company funds to further private interests.[25]

The 1912 congressional Money Trust Investigation into the concentration of control of money and credit conducted by the Pujo committee also probed into conflict of interest. The investment banker J. P. Morgan was questioned by Samuel Untermyer, counsel of the Pujo committee, about situations in which investment bankers, as voting trustees, named the directors and selected themselves as fiscal agents: "Don't you feel that in a sense, when it comes to issuing securities of that company and fixing the prices on which they are to be issued, that you are in a sense dealing with yourselves?" Morgan disagreed: "I do not think so. We do not deal with ourselves."[26] But when George W. Perkins was asked "Would you consider it proper for directors with advance information of the condition of a company to deal in its stock?" he drew the line: "I do not."[27]

The Pujo committee also scrutinized the precise relations of officers and directors to their banks. Two separate issues were involved: the ability to borrow from the bank and the ability to participate in a security underwriting in which the bank either was or might be participating.

George M. Reynolds, president of the Continental and Commercial National Bank of Chicago, contended that although both were legal, loans to officers were improper (and not made by his bank) but loans to directors were not. Reynolds also stated that he was neither a director nor a stockholder in any concern that dealt with his bank and that this was true of the other officers as well: "I felt I would be free and untrammeled and would exercise the dictates of my own conscience more freely, and that it would at least prove good faith to the public so far as my conduct of the business would be concerned." Jacob H. Schiff of Kuhn, Loeb agreed with Reynolds that directors should not borrow from their own banks in their personal capacity, but he approved the practice when it was done on behalf of a business in which they were interested. Henry P. Davison of J. P. Morgan and Company concurred that officers should not borrow from their banks but held that this limitation did not apply to directors. The Pujo committee recommended that officers be prohibited from borrowing from their banks but reluctantly conceded that this prohibition should not apply to directors.[28]

Another variant of conflict of interest occurred in the underwriting of security issues by banks. Davison objected to bank officers serving as participants in an underwriting in which the bank itself was a participant; he denied that he had ever been on either end of such a transaction. Robert Winsor (Kidder, Peabody, & Company) was also opposed to giving participations to officers of banks that were or might be participating in an underwriting. But Francis L. Hine, president of the First National Bank of New York, took the opposite view, defending as morally correct the participation of bank officers in underwritings when the bank was an actual or potential customer.[29]

The Pujo committee recommended that both officers and directors of banks be prohibited from participating in underwriting operations in which their banks were or might become interested.[30] (This practice had been allowed in the life insurance field prior to the Armstrong investigation but was made illegal thereafter.) This participation in underwriting can probably be construed to be the accepted morality by 1913. Certainly the thrust of the evolving morality was to prohibit the conflict of interest, but the use of security affiliates represented a skillful evasion of the principle. The legality, and for that matter the morality, of this form of business behavior was not finally settled until the Banking Act of 1933 divorced security affiliates from commercial banking. There is perhaps less moral fault if banking was regarded purely as a private business for private profit than if looked on as involving important public obligations.

Conflict of interest diminished, in part, as a result of public exposure, although other forces, including legislation at the state level in the wake of investigations, were also responsible. The exposure of the life insurance business by the Armstrong investigation and subsequent legislation established a new standard of business behavior, severing the connection between the major life insurance companies and the investment community, and there was noticeably less conflict of interest in this industry thereafter. The prohibition by the Clayton Act (1914) of interlocking directorates and directorships acted against conflict of interest, as well as concentration of power in the hands of the few. Furthermore, businessmen generally were cognizant of the publicity that had thrust the activities of the leaders of the business community into the limelight. There is little doubt that during the Progressive Era the conventional morality on conflict of interest was redefined. Self-interest as a guide to action was no longer permitted if it involved a conflict of interest.

The source of change was mostly external in the course of this period; the public conscience was aroused not only by the behavior of businessmen but also by their failure to offer a plausible account of their actions. Surely George W. Perkins was not the same man after he underwent cross-examination during the Armstrong investigation that he had been before; his integrity had been challenged and his psyche had not emerged from the confrontation unscathed. Businessmen must internalize the views and values of the community in order to avoid conflict with it. Since they did not in this instance, the representatives of the electorate defined the new morality through the legislative process. The disagreements among the insiders, and between insiders and outsiders, culminated in improved business morality. All segments of society ultimately would agree on the appropriate direction.

RESTRAINT OF TRADE

The growth of large-scale enterprises proceeded at a remarkable rate around the turn of the century. This seemingly inevitable movement involved two distinct conditions: big business and monopolistic business. Big business is defined by sheer size, achieved either through internal or external (via merger) growth. Monopolistic business refers to the share of the market held by the top one, two, three, or four firms; monopolistic power even may be exercised by firms that are not large compared either to others in the industry or to the economy as a whole. Both conditions are intimately associated, but they are not identical.

By 1914 the concentration ratios of many major industries were such that in each the four (or fewer) largest firms produced enough of the total output to dominate the industry. As rational oligopolists, such firms did not necessarily employ traditional means such as price agreements. Sometimes they obtained their ends through administered prices, principally price leadership. Although the variety of means increased, the end remained the same. Competition among the few was more prevalent by 1914 than it had been earlier, and restraint of trade through price agreements diminished.

A unique form of restraint of trade occurred following the invention of the Owens bottling machine in 1903. The machine was licensed to bottle manufacturers; each manufacturer had an exclusive license for particular types of ware, with production quotas for each type, and the Owens Bottle Machine Company retained control over the prices charged by the bottle manufacturers it licensed.[31] (This industry ultimately was investigated by a congressional committee and was an unsuccessful defendant in an antitrust suit for just these actions.) A more conventional form of restraint of trade is exemplified by the Western Shipping Brewers' Association, which was organized in 1898 and dissolved in 1912. Its members achieved the same ends of price protection and the preservation of customer relationship through fear of retaliation by competitors.[32] In a rational oligopoly no one needs to be told not to cut prices.

Herman Sielcken devised a remarkable scheme in his coffee control plan, which was designed to limit the production of coffee and hold the surplus off the market for sale at higher prices. Sielcken was one of the coffee dealers who arranged the plan and the financing. Since the plan relied on crop control by the Brazilian government that did not materialize, this effort failed.[33]

Agreements, implied or expressed, to suspend or curtail the force of competition flourished in this era in a number of sectors of the economy. Some investment bankers did not compete for business where an established client-banker relationship existed.[34] One such investment banker, Jacob H. Schiff (Kuhn, Loeb & Company), testified before the Pujo committee that business ethics did not permit one house to compete for the business of another with an established client or customer.[35]

Henry P. Davison, a member of the firm of J. P. Morgan and Company, reported that it was a matter of banking ethics for the same banks to participate in an additional security issue for a company if a previous issue for the same company with the same banking participants was satisfactory. Francis L. Hine (First National) agreed: "The same ethics obtain in banking that obtain in the legal profession and in the medical profession, as to preserves of other. . . . It is the custom—I am not dealing in ethics." Banking ethics or business morals required that if any of the participants received an issue, it handled the issue for the joint account. This practice obviously restricted the range of choice for companies seeking investment banking services.[36]

J. P. Morgan and Company, in its reply to the Pujo committee, asserted that although competitive bidding was not used by corporations in the marketing of securities, there was no evidence that any corporation failed to receive the best possible price.[37] Yet this statement by the most powerful investment banker of the time failed to deal with either the conflict-of-interest issue or the absence of competition through implicit, if not explicit, agreement. The conflict of interest was inherent because the investment banker frequently had a representative on the board of directors of the issuing company and therefore was able to act as both buyer and seller.

The Pujo investigation also examined an unusual form of price agreement, inaugurated in 1899 by the New York Clearing House Association. The association began to require that its member banks impose uniform collection charges on out-of-town checks, although clearinghouses functionally have nothing to do with out-of-town check collection. Member banks had to maintain rates or face expulsion from the clearinghouse. This practice eliminated price competition and prohibited banks from treating each customer according to the value of the account.

The committee had to examine two questions. First, was an agreement on collection charges an agreement in restraint of trade? Samuel Untermyer, counsel of the Pujo committee, charged that it was. But James G. Cannon, president of the Fourth National Bank of New York, denied this. Waldo E. Newcomer, president of the National Exchange Bank of Baltimore and also president of the Baltimore Clearing House, testified that he did not think free competition on collection charges in the banking business should be allowed. Frank A. Vanderlip, president of the National City Bank, agreed with both Cannon and Newcomer: "I do not recognize any vice in the matter."[38]

The second question was whether an agreement on collection

charges was necessary in the banking business. Testifying that it was not, Alfred C. Knox of the Mellon National Bank of Pittsburgh felt that allowing each bank to set its own collection charges, as in the Pittsburgh Clearing House Association, worked well. Knox's bank charged each customer in accordance with the value of the account; thus some customers were charged and some were not. Francis B. Reeves, president of the Philadelphia Clearing House Association and of the Girard National Bank, noted that the Philadelphia association had no rules on charges for the collection of out-of-town checks.[39]

Thus the spectrum of behavior on charges on out-of-town collections varied from one clearinghouse to another. The dichotomy was between equal treatment for all and restraint of trade. There is a conflict between two apparently irreconcilable principles: some sort of agreement by sellers or discrimination among buyers. As a purely practical business proposition, these two principles cannot be reconciled without government intervention.

The anthracite coal industry devised its own restraint-of-trade practices. The industry continued to be plagued by excess capacity, but it was favored by the existence of conditions appropriate for combination. From 1898 to 1914, railroad consolidation, the development of a community of interest among the railroads, and the practical elimination of the independent mine operators characterized the industry. Directly or indirectly, the anthracite railroads owned or controlled 90 percent of the output of anthracite coal.[40] The community of interest raised freight rates for anthracite, discriminated against independent coal operators, and lifted prices; at the same time it stabilized output, lowered costs, and increased efficiency.[41] In order to achieve market control and to forestall the creation of an independent road, the anthracite roads allocated shares of the market to themselves. Collusion among the various railroads, with the Reading acting as price leader, fixed the price of anthracite coal.[42]

Testifying before the industrial Commission in 1901, E. B. Thomas, president of the Erie Railroad Company, denied the existence of an anthracite combination, but he added:"Now, as to community of interest, we do consult together. It is impossible to

conduct the commercial affairs of this country without consulta-
tion. There are no agreements, express or implied."[43] But even if
there was no collusion, the market structure was such that the
same oligopolistic results were achieved through other means.

The common-law opposition to railroad pooling had been
supplemented by a statutory prohibition in the Interstate Commerce
Act of 1887. Senator Shelby Cullom did not want the prohibition
in the act of 1887 but accepted it in exchange for a liberalized
long-short-haul clause, that is, charging more for carrying freight
a short distance than a longer one.[44] Largely responsible for the
form the law took, Cullom wrote in 1911 on pooling, "Whether it
is right or wrong, I do not know even to this day."[45] Considering
the complexities of the issue and the ultimate reversal in the Transportation Act of 1920, his comment reflects a legitimate bewilder-
ment.

Diverse views existed as to the meaning of restraint of trade and
from the passage of the Sherman Antitrust Act in 1890 to the
Northern Securities decision in 1904, public policy remained
uncertain in purpose and ineffective in operation. Pooling agreements had been generally unenforceable under common law
before 1890 although the courts had been less rigorously opposed
to railroad pooling than in other industries. Moreover, the federal
government had not instituted legal proceedings regarding pooling.
Industrial pools after 1890 had questionable legal status, but it
was unclear if the Sherman Antitrust Act applied to manufacturing
because the decisions of the Supreme Court in interpreting and
applying the law to business enterprises and their behavior did
not consistently point in one direction.

The decision in the E. C. Knight case (1895) convinced business
that combinations in manufacturing would not be molested despite the Sherman Act. The Addyston Pipe case (1899) dealt with
a price agreement in interstate commerce, and this was ruled illegal
as a violation of the Sherman Act.[46] If these two cases offered any
generalizations at all, business could infer that close combinations,
in which the competitors disappeared through a merger were legal,
but loose combinations, which used price agreements, were illegal.
The judgment of business that the Sherman Act was of no consequence was confirmed by the failure of government to prosecute

after the Knight case and by the generally favorable attitude of government toward big business. This may help to explain certain actions and beliefs of businessmen.[47]

In the light of this situation, it is not surprising that Andrew Carnegie was able to be nonchalant about the Sherman Antitrust Act in the 1890s. "Do you really expect men engaged in an active struggle to make a living at manufacturing to be posted about laws and their decisions, and what is applied here, there, and everywhere?"[48] he asked in his testimony in 1912 before the Stanley committee investigation of U.S. Steel. Similarly, Carnegie commented on the failure of counsel to inform him about public policy concerning restraint of trade: "Nobody ever mentioned the Sherman Act to me, that I remember."[49]

Some businessmen, however, regarded the law prohibiting agreements by persons to fix prices seriously. Owens Bottle removed price-fixing clauses from its leases in 1911 because of fear of the law and stopped leasing but still tied a series of machines.[50] The Du Pont Company acquired and consolidated its competitors partly in order to accomplish "avoidance of trade agreements contrary to law," according to an internal report prepared in 1904 by Pierre S. du Pont. He "insisted that the legal and moral dangers of continued use of separate companies and trade agreements far outweighed their benefits." The organization of the consolidated Du Pont Company effectively terminated the Gunpowder Trade Association, which was a loose combination designed to fix prices, allocate markets, and stabilize profits. Despite the replacement of a loose combination by a close one, the Du Pont Company lost an antitrust suit in 1911 following the Standard Oil and American Tobacco decisions, and dissolution resulted.[51] Similarly, the Ammunition Manufacturers Association was dissolved in 1907.[52] By this time, after the antimonopolistic Addyston Pipe and Steel Company decision, businessmen had ample opportunity to become convinced of something that would not have concerned them two decades earlier: restraint of trade or monopolistic behavior might well be illegal.

Not all businesses responded to the growing significance of the antitrust law as interpreted by the courts by consolidating. As the public became increasingly concerned with combination, many businessmen became increasingly convinced that such combinations were essential. Such firms tried to evade the law either through secrecy or through the use of a means that, while more concerned with form than substance, would be legal. An executive of Bucyrus (an excavating machinery manufacturer) visited its principal competitor, Marion Steam Shovel, and reported to his company on the attitude of a Marion man.

Cheney also said they had always felt disposed to act in a friendly attitude toward us, while he admitted that both sides had gone after each other's friends [customers]. . . Cheney . . . said that we should certainly arrange in some manner [so that] they could bid high to our friends and vice versa. . . . "Of course," he said, "any agreement would have to be verbal . . . and would have to be lived up to by both parties."[53]

Similarly the steel industry during the early twentieth century used different means to restrain what it considered to be the ill effects of competition. Following the organization of United States Steel in 1901, pooling agreements and trade meetings were used. They were superseded by the Gary dinners, first held in 1907 and ended in 1911. Gary dinners were "friendly" affairs among competitors in which they could discuss business conditions. Elbert H. Gary was the head of United States Steel, the largest firm in the industry, with about half the total output. The Gary dinners and the meetings that followed used no agreements, quotas, or penalties because such devices were illegal under the Sherman Antitrust Act. Instead there was a general understanding as to prices, and United States Steel became the price leader. Deviations were considered immoral; honor demanded both agreement and compliance with the agreement.[54] The individual businessman was therefore faced with a conflict of loyalties between the law or universal ethic and the particular ethic of his colleagues in the industry.

A great merger wave around the turn of the century resulted in the consolidation of business on an unprecedented scale. Big business dominated an increasing number of industries. The large companies became still larger. Popular concern mounted and altered the stance of the federal government. The Northern Securities case (1904) destroyed the idea that close combinations effected through formally organized holding companies were not as vulnerable to the Sherman Act as any other type of combination. That decision was, in turn, modified by the rule of reason of the Standard Oil case (1911), which resulted in the dissolution of Standard Oil, although the Supreme Court recognized that not all combinations were an illegal restraint of trade. Certainly the muckraking journals during the Progressive Era made a broad cross-section of the population conscious of the significance of restraint of trade, and businessmen had to include the Sherman Act in their calculations, even if they did not always see the moral implications of power.

There appears to have been little alteration in the morality of businessmen with respect to restraint of trade during the Progressive Era. The courts did inaugurate a new policy of interpretation with the Northern Securities and Standard Oil cases. Furthermore, the representatives of the electorate indicated their acceptance of a shift in business morality by the enactment of the Clayton Antitrust Act (1914), which futher limited the means by which restraint of trade could be achieved. The Federal Trade Commission Act (1914) also pointed to a concern with monopoly abuses. With both the Standard Oil and American Tobacco cases decided in the same year (the former according to the rule of reason, condemning an unreasonable restraint of trade), businessmen could no longer be oblivious to the moral aspect of restraint of trade, and certain practices did become violations of the antitrust laws. These decisions permitted size (especially if generated through internal growth), economies of scale, and oligopoly but denied the ethical propriety of unreasonable restraint of trade. Nonetheless, the business community did not treat those convicted as pariahs. The means underwent a revision but the ends did not, and there were probably few businessmen attached to large-scale enterprises who subscribed to a new moral code. Such change as did occur in the morality of restraint of trade was largely prompted by external impulses.

COMPETITIVE TACTICS

Other competitive tactics pursued by business were not essentially new, but they continued to be applied with unrelenting vigor even if frequently on a reduced scale. To lower either cost or price was so vital in winning a competitive advantage that there was constant pressure at the outer limits of morality.

Railroad freight rate discrimination, a prime competitive tactic, had been in vogue especially since the depression of 1873.[55] As the evidence presented to the Industrial Commission at the turn of the century fully demonstrated, railroad freight rate discrimination as to persons (shippers) did not cease following the creation of the Interstate Commerce Commission. Many shippers and railroads obeyed the letter of the law, but they used evasive techniques and sought loopholes, with the occasional resulting legal costs and fines charged to shipping costs. The commission was generally ineffective; many railroad men urged the adoption of an effective law because rate cutting and discrimination reduced revenues.[56] The Elkins Act (1903) made receiving as well as granting rebates illegal, thereby making both shipper and carrier accountable, and it also prohibited any deviation from the public rate. Rebating persisted, however, although on a lesser scale, because of the manner in which the courts interpreted this law.[57] Subsequent legislation—the Hepburn Act (1906) and the Mann-Elkins Act (1910)—strengthened government regulation although even this approach failed to achieve universal compliance.[58]

Two giant corporations were arraigned before the bar of justice and public opinion during the second administration of the trust-buster, Theodore Roosevelt. The Garfield Report of 1906 alleged railroad discrimination in favor of Standard Oil, and the main charges were valid in the sense that the oil company had seized upon legal loopholes. The dominant oil firm and the railroads cancelled some of the alleged discriminatory rates but not until sued in major cases. Although Standard's legal position was strong and it contended that it obeyed the law as it then existed, Standard's actions appeared to constitute legal evasion, and therefore its public position was weak. The possibility of generalized legal action instituted by a multitude of governments for diverse reasons hung over the heads of the executives of large-scale enterprises, especially Standard Oil's.[59] As an indication that the new federal laws against rebating were effectively enforced, the New York Central was found guilty of giving rebates to American Sugar Refining in 1907.[60]

William Z. Ripley, a professor of economics and one of the outstanding railroad experts of this period, commented: "The most
important result of this Federal activity so far, has been the moral
stimulus toward fair business dealing which has been given. Thousands of shippers today, quite apart from the fear of fines or im-
prisonment, would disdain to ask or accept favors which a decade
since would have been regarded as entirely proper."[61]

Discrimination as to persons continued to plague the life insurance companies as it had troubled the railroads. The life insurance
business entered the new century in the midst of the keenest kind
of competition. Each of the Big Three still desired to be the largest,
and the smaller companies copied their practices since all were
striving to increase the amount of insurance in force. In their
quest for growth, the life insurance companies typically sold
tontine policies and paid high commission to salesmen who attracted
new business. They also commonly engaged in rebating, twisting—
that is, inducing a policy holder to switch an existing policy from
one company to another—and raiding in order to obtain a competitive advantage. The rebates paid to customers by the agents
depended on the high commissions paid to obtain new business;
the higher the commissions, the more of a problem was rebating.[62]
Although insurance men frequently deplored these practices, the
early laws against them were relatively ineffective, and the industry, in a supplementary action, attempted voluntary cooperation
in 1895 to suppress rebating. Equitable reduced first-year commissions in 1899 in an unsuccessful effort to implement this agreement
but then withdrew from it.[63] This was indeed the crux of the moral
dilemma. Jacob L. Greene of Connecticut Mutual opposed rebating,
and his firm suffered from the rebating of the Big Three.[64]

Company policy tended to be opposed to rebating, but agents
violated the rule; the morality of top management had not been
internalized at the agent's level. Despite the passage by New York
of an antirebate law in 1889, the practice persisted, and John A.
McCall (New York Life) told the Armstrong committee that he
had dismissed "quite a number of agents" for violations of the law.
Equitable as of 1893 had made a reasonable effort to comply.[65]
Northwestern Mutual officers told the Wisconsin insurance investigation that rebating could not be stopped unless the man-

agement of all life insurance companies refused to accept a policy if the agent paid a rebate. Perhaps as a consequence, Wisconsin in 1911 enacted a law penalizing policy holders who accepted a rebate by reducing the amount of their coverage proportionately.[66] Yet, rebating continued, though on a decreased scale.[67] The life insurance companies vacillated and did not consistently adhere to an internal policy of opposition and rigid enforcement.

The New York State investigation revolutionized the life insurance business. Quite correctly, it focused on the behavior of the three companies that provided the leadership (in 1890 the Big Three had almost 50 percent of the legal reserve life insurance in force), but some small companies were equally guilty.[68]

The Armstrong investigation introduced a new ethical era for life insurance. Top management of the large insurance companies resigned and was replaced in its wake.[69] The Armstrong committee uncovered the abuses. Life insurance rebating had been related to the high commissions paid agents, which, in turn, were linked to raiding of each other's agents by the Big Three in their quest for preeminence and by their competitors in their push for sales volume. Subsequent legislation ended the competitive race for growth, prohibited tontine policies (discontinued previously by some smaller firms such as Northwestern although continued by other companies outside New York for some time), and regulated other activities.[70] The reform movement strengthened the hands of the more moral life insurance executives and companies. Additional internal changes, principally brought about by some officers, aided in the moral change. As Henry L. Palmer, president of Northwestern Mutual, said during the Wisconsin life insurance investigation, "The Company may have outgrown the methods which suited it in the past."[71] This was true not only of this company but also of the industry generally. Yet despite the aftermath of the Armstrong investigation, questionable practices outlived this era. Probably the most marked alteration in this industry that derived from these reforms was the relative decline of the Big Three.[72]

One of the achievements of the Progressive Era was that it stirred the public consciousness in many different directions. The quality of products was one area. The patent medicine manufacturers were possibly the largest users of advertising space in newspapers and certainly the largest national advertisers in 1900.[73] Within a decade the industry was reduced to much more modest proportions. In the nineties Dr. Oliver Wendell Holmes and his colleagues had condemned patent medicine men for pretending to be physicians when they were not, fabricating testimonials, inventing nonexistent diseases, claiming the product was foreign in origin, faking statistical evidence, claiming cures for diseases that could not be cured at all, and claiming quick cures for diseases that could not be cured quickly. The articles in such popular periodicals as the *Ladies' Home Journal* of 1904 and *Collier's Weekly* the next year alerted an influential segment of the lay public to the social aspects of advertising. Rural newspapers usually carried patent medicine advertising (William Allen White's *Emporia Gazette* was a notable exception). Even as late as 1905 medical journals, including the *Journal of the American Medical Association*, carried patent medicine advertising.[74] After 1905 N. W. Ayer, a leading advertising agency, refused to place any patent medicine advertising.[75] Even the proprietary medicine manufacturers, as a result of the change in public sentiment, were ready to accept restrictive legislation when the Pure Food and Drug Act was passed in 1906.[76] Various groups of manufacturers welcomed the act as a curb on the competitive practices of some of their competitors.

Retailers supplemented the efforts of manufacturers by advertising also. Sears, Roebuck, for example, advertised patent medicines extensively in its catalog. In 1905, William Pettigrew, who had joined Sears two years earlier, was assigned the task of preparing the patent medicine copy for the catalog. Pettigrew was, in his own words, "shocked." He declined to do the assignment again on the grounds that the patent medicine business was thoroughly dishonest. The Pure Food and Drug Act changed matters, by prohibiting adulterated or fraudently labled foods and drugs, but Montgomery Ward in its fall 1909–1910 catalog featured a more limited presentation of drugs and patent medicines than did Sears, which began to pursue the same policy in 1911. Sears stopped selling some products, and its advertising copy for the rest was less extravagant. By 1913 Sears discontinued the sale of patent medicines. Ward's continued to sell them, but the products were more selective and the presentations were on the conservative side.[77]

The problem of quality control existed in products other than drugs. Sears, Roebuck did not know the contents of the fabrics that were used to make the men's suits that it bought, and this was true of other products as well. In a letter to a Sears executive in 1908, Richard Sears remarked that the old methods of merchandising were not bad for the time but that now better ethics must prevail. Sears, Roebuck established a testing laboratory in 1911 to bring its merchandise within the spirit of the Pure Food and Drug Act. The public generally, the advertising business, and the periodical press all wanted more truthful advertising.[78]

Promotion or advertising certainly did not exhaust the possible means by which large-scale enterprises attempted to obtain a competitive edge. In the suit that resulted in the dissolution of Standard Oil in 1911, Standard Oil was charged with the use of such competitive practices as local price cutting, bogus companies, reporting on competitors' shipments, and rebates to favored buyers. M. F. Elliott, who in 1905 succeeded S. C. T. Dodd as Standard's principal counsel, had advised against the use of "hidden" or "bogus" companies since 1898, but he cited no legal references and the practice continued. Archbold and other Standard Oil executives still considered such practices legal when Standard Oil abandoned their use in 1906 in response to public pressure. The adverse publicity in the muckraking press impelled one Du Pont Company executive in 1903 to send another a piece from *McClure's* on Standard Oil's competitive tactics and cautioned against the use of such methods lest external protest be provoked.[79]

Other companies and men utilized secrecy in different ways. Minnesota Mining and Manufacturing kept secret the true value of its mine property. The company implied that the land contained a mineral supposedly useful for abrasive purposes in sandpaper but which was actually worthless for the purpose. An R. G. Dun credit report of 1910 was based on the presumption that the mineral was valuable; three years later another credit report admitted that it was worthless.[80] An equally interesting illustration of the use of secrecy was employed by Alexander R. Malcomsen, Ford's backer in the Ford Motor Company. Malcomsen invested in Ford's predecessor concern in 1902 but required that the banks not be notified of this additional obligation (he was heavily in debt because of overexpansion of other business ventures).[81] And Edward D. Libbey of Owens Bottle Company in 1903 tried to negotiate with a group of beer bottle manufacturers for the exclusive use of the Owens bottle machine. The group could not agree among themselves, so Libbey approached one of the members of the group and concluded an agreement. The others learned of this and claimed that they had been betrayed.[82]

Secrecy was now a matter of controversy within business.[83] Whereas it had been the traditional general rule, now the rule had an increasing number of exceptions, and the controversy arose from the necessity of deciding what information to make public and when. Competitive business sanctioned the use of secrecy but in a more limited sense than previously. James J. Hill (Great Northern) opposed cumulative voting (multiple votes for a single nominee and none for others) for the directors of corporations on the grounds that secrecy was sometimes necessary in business operations. "You know a railroad in order to get its right of way has got to do it quietly."[84] John D. Archbold, president of Standard Oil (New Jersey), was opposed to making stockholder lists public, and Standard did this only when it realized that the law made publication mandatory.[85]

Local price cutting was defended by Livingston Roe, a Standard Oil executive, in a statement to Far East agents in 1902: "It is our practice at home to regulate our selling prices in the various territories in the U.S, with regard to the competition we are meeting in each particular place, and to make up in one place for the sacrifices we are obliged to make in others."[86] Competitors arrived at a consensus as to what represented fair competition, and the same methods tended to be used widely, becoming the universalistic ethic of the oil industry.

By 1914 the competitive tactics sanctioned by the dominant business morality, the universalistic ethic, were quite different from what they had been as recently as 1900. The principal explanation for this quiet revolution seems to be external: the passage of appropriate legislation, frequently, but not invariably, at the federal level.

Railroad freight rate discrimination was not as widespread

in 1900 as it had been a generation or more before. Railroad mileage approached its apogee. The consolidation of major railroads into half a dozen communities of interest by the early twentieth century virtually eliminated rate cutting even before the Hepburn Act.[87] Communities of interest, in conjunction with effective federal regulation, ended the long-festering problem of railroad freight rate discrimination as between persons and facilitated the impartial treatment of shippers to the satisfaction of many railroad leaders, but, as discrimination ended, rates rose.[88] The Elkins Act (1903), the Hepburn Act (1906), and the Mann-Elkins Act (1910) strengthened the regulation of the railroads and made the rebate a matter of historic interest rather than an objective of traffic managers. Subject to detailed public regulation, railroads continued to compete, but no longer on the basis of price. Shippers came to regard only the open, posted price as morally acceptable.

The life insurance industry received a thorough airing by legislative investigations in New York and Wisconsin. Although the enactment of corrective legislation by the various states did not totally eliminate some marketing methods, it did significantly modify the competitive tactics employed in this industry. It is also likely that the leaders of this industry underwent a certain amount of attitude change as a result of their ordeal of publicity.

A similar process was at work in the marketing of a variety of consumer products. Patent medicines, heretofore an important article of commerce, were regulated by the Pure Food and Drug Act (1906), a law that applied to other products as well and induced businessmen to reexamine their business morality. Some adopted policies even stricter than those mandated by the law.

Finally, the Clayton Antitrust Act (1914) forbade discrimination in prices between purchasers when the effect was "to substantially lessen competition or tend to create a monopoly." It also plugged a loophole in the Sherman Act uncovered as a result of certain court decisions, when it prohibited exclusive selling or leasing contracts of both patented and unpatented articles. Both of these provisions circumscribed the ability of the leading firms to erect barriers to the entry of potential competitors in their industries.

Essentially courts and legislatures defined what constituted acceptable competitive business morality. This process of definition involved outlawing certain business practices of long standing. Some pressures for the change were internal to the firms, as indicated by selective business support for some legislation, such as the Federal Trade Commission Act (1914).[89] Some pressures were external, and intervention by government was of profound influence in evoking a new business morality, a higher universalistic ethic. It was, however, of little consequence in the sale of watered stock.

STOCK WATERING

During the Progressive Era, the public, both as investors and customers, continued to be concerned about the morality of stock watering, which had been common since the 1850s. According to academic investment analysts writing later and from the perspective of fundamentalist outsider investors, watered stock involved rank, deliberate deception as to the asset values "existing behind the shares."[90] Insiders who practiced stock watering were not troubled by it.[91]

The battle over watered stock continued to rage during the early twentieth century, and new incidents provided further ammunition. One episode that especially agitated the combatants was E. H. Harriman's reorganization of the Chicago & Alton Railroad. Harriman acquired control of this road in 1898, the line invested a substantial sum of money in physical improvements with a beneficial effect on earnings, and the Alton declared a stock dividend. During the Progressive Era though, the Alton was held up as an egregious example of stock watering by critics of big business who did not understand the intricacies of the financial details.[92]

Defenders of stock watering in railroads contended that owners had the right to all earnings in whatever forms and denied the existence of a link between capitalization and rates. Robert S. Lovett (Union Pacific) testified in 1910:

I feel entirely warranted in stating that the railroad rates, both passenger and freight, prevailing throughout the United States today were not made, and were not in any wise influenced, by the stocks and bonds outstanding, and that the needs of the companies for interest on bonds and dividends on stock had nothing whatever to do with the fixing of the rates.

The Industrial Commission concurred that stock watering had no direct connection with railroad rates.[93] In this context stock watering was really a sterile issue. Nevertheless, the opponents (the general public and the public's agents, the regulatory commissions) usually assumed the contrary. They charged that capitalization had an indirect influence on the general level of rates because there was a positive incentive for higher rates to support a large capitalization. Some regulatory commissions (although not the Interstate Commerce Commission under Thomas M. Cooley) reasoned that, although initially railroads set rates that yielded the maximum return regardless of capitalization, ultimately other criteria determined the reasonableness of rates.

Several railroads were involved in stock watering and out of these episodes came public regulation, first at the state level and later nationally. Massachusetts had regulated railroad security issues even prior to creating its railroad commission in 1869. At that juncture Massachusetts added further restrictions and then in 1894 prohibited railroads from adding new stock to capitalization except at market value of the stock in a further effort to cope with stock watering. Even in this state, which had a strong tradition of restrictive regulation, the consensus dictated the enactment of a more liberalized law in 1907, allowing new issues of capital stock to be sold below market but no lower than par value.[94] Texas checked overcapitalization in 1893 by requiring that no new railroad securities be issued without the approval of a public authority.[95] And the Mann-Elkins Act (1910), with its investigatory provision, expressed the concern of the federal government with watered stock.[96] (Eventually the Transportation Act of 1920 gave the Interstate Commerce Commission full and exclusive control of security issues by interstate railroads.) By the time that railroad capitalization was effectively controlled, the railroad building age was over, but legislation was passed to cope with the capitalization-rate issue by using a value other than capitalization as a yardstick for rates.

Overcapitalization was not confined to railroads. United States

Steel accomplished stock watering by overstating the value of its tangible assets. And F. W. Woolworth employed another principal means by using goodwill as an intangible asset and carrying it on the books at an arbitrary figure. Only sporadically, as in the case of the investigation of United States Steel, did stock watering among industrials come to the fore as a public isue.

One of the relatively rare occasions when the capitalization of an industrial concern came to public attention occurred in 1907 when the Bureau of Corporations issued a report on prices and profits in the petroleum industry in which it claimed that Standard Oil's profits were excessive. Standard Oil defended itself in a publicity release by contending that the profits were not excessive if properties, goodwill, and managerial capacity were fully capitalized.[97] Once again the same question arose: What should be included in capitalization? The rate of profit would look high or low depending on the elements included. In this case Standard Oil had not watered its stock; it was actually undercapitalized, and it argued correctly that this fact overstated its rate of profit.

Liberal doses of water were typically added to the capitalization of the industrial combinations, such as United States Steel, assembled during the great merger wave around the turn of the century. One combination with only a limited amount of water was the International Harvester Company, organized in 1902. The price paid by the new company for the physical properties of the merged companies was set before the appraisal, which substantially exceeded the purchase price. Still, about 15 percent of the capitalization was water because the value of the fixed assets was inflated. Nonetheless, in comparison with other such promotions of the same vintage, this one was conservative.[98]

The conservative McCormick brothers opposed stock watering in the McCormick Harvesting Machine Company, the closely-held, family-owned company.[99] During the negotiations leading to the formation of International Harvester, George W. Perkins, a Morgan partner, told the McCormick brothers that J. P. Morgan and Company was in general opposed to stock watering but that it was sometimes necessary when prospective companies made excessive demands.[100] William Nelson Cromwell, a noted corporation lawyer, told the McCormick brothers that Morgan watered

stock to increase his profits.[101] This, and perhaps their own knowledge of such previous Morgan-sponsored combinations as United
States Steel, made the McCormicks afraid of Morgan's renown
for watering stock.[102]

Watered stock continued to generate a broad spectrum of comment. The principal new ingredient was the spread of stock watering and the argument concerning it from the railroads to other
unregulated sectors of the economy. Watered stock as it applied
to the railroads ceased to be an issue with the passage of the Valuation Act (1913), which severed the traditional relationship between
capitalization, profits, and rates. Before World War I the assets
were of at least as much importance as earnings were in valuing a
business, although many American businessmen by the turn of
the century advocated the use of earning power as the basis for
capitalization. Perhaps the legalization of no par value stock in
1912 by New York State and the more or less simultaneous investigation of United States Steel show the awareness of the issue
as it applied to industry generally. During the 1920s, assets became unimportant for valuing securities, as earnings became all
important. By the time the so-called Securities Acts of 1933–1934
were passed, watered stock had historical rather than current
significance.[103]

In this case, therefore, it was not an improvement in business
morality that took place but an improvement in the good sense
of businessmen's critics.

Legislation covering watered stock in the industrial sector was
not placed on the statute books until the New Deal. "Goodwill,"
the common way of watering stock at one time, vanished, leaving
only a trace as "purchased goodwill."[104]

FINANCIAL REPORTING

Financial reporting remained in a somewhat primitive state at the
turn of the century. As the economy became more complex, as
the scale of enterprise grew, as the number of stockholders proliferated, and as the role of government as a regulator of the
economy expanded, the need for adequate financial reporting
inspired new and more stringent demands on management. Man-

agement itself required improved financial reporting as a means of controlling the farflung activities of the multiproduct, multi-divisional enterprises for which the old-fashioned rule of thumb had formerly sufficed. Investors and the general public were interested in two separate and yet related aspects of financial reports: the availability of information and the reliability of information.

At the turn of the century, when the first of the annual Moody's manuals was published, the management of the very few publicly owned manufacturing corporations disclosed little financial information to outsiders, and the published material on corporations was usually tainted with "sins of omission."[105] Some companies, large as well as small, provided no reports at all. The management was unwilling to furnish the general public, or even the stockholders, with financial statements; for example, the president of the Smith and Griggs Manufacturing Company, a small brass fabricator, provided even such insiders as the directors with little information and acted as a proprietary manager.[106] Such secrecy was characteristic of small and closely-held manufacturers. Typically manufacturing companies provided financial reports with limited detail—perhaps a handful of asset accounts and an equal number of liability accounts but no profit and loss statement. Several corporate giants issued more detailed financial reports, possibly because of their heavy reliance on the capital market or their adoption of a long-term view.

Regulated industries constituted a different category. Public utilities, insurance companies, banks, and railroads were commonly compelled to submit some form of financial report to the appropriate regulatory agency. The railroads had been obliged under section 20 of the Interstate Commerce Act of 1887 (and earlier state legislation) to supply accounting reports, but some railroads failed to comply, and the courts sustained them. However, Kidder, Peabody and Company, one of the foremost investment banking firms, as part of the price of its financial assistance, stipulated in 1888 that the Santa Fe institute the "uniform railroad bookkeeping system," modeled on that of the Pennsylvania.[107] The Hepburn Act of 1906 made the provision of this information mandatory, required standardized reports, and also gave the Interstate Commerce Commission the power to inspect railroad books. An unsuccessful attempt was made in 1908 to nullify the intent of this clause of the Hepburn Act, but it was halted by the efforts of Theodore Roosevelt.[108] State legislation, administered by a special department, directed life insurance companies to file reports.

Financial reporting as it existed early in the twentieth century needed considerable improvement. The concept of depreciation was not clearly understood by some professional accountants. Depreciation was not common even after the turn of the century, and the amount charged varied with the fortunes of the company.[109] Some firms charged it to the value of the asset or underestimated the amount. Depreciation was introduced increasingly when companies merged in an effort to achieve accounting comparability for all parts of the new, and inherently more difficult to manage, concern.

Until the Interstate Commerce Commission regulations of 1907 required depreciation accounting, the practice of replacement (or renewal) accounting was almost universal by railroads. Replacement accounting meant that equipment replacements were charged to current operating expenses at the time expenditures were made, and no entry ever appeared in the capital account. By charging repairs to operating expenses, railroads, which had a high proportion of fixed to total cost, inflated operating costs and deflated capital consumption.[110]

Management also had several alternative ways of treating the profit and loss account. On occasion, nonrecurring expenses were deducted from surplus, while nonrecurring income was added to profit. If this was done and concealed from the public, then profits could be inflated. Assets were also inflated to impress unwary investors, and watered stock was offset by goodwill. Therefore securities would be more marketable than otherwise would have been the case. The United States Steel annual report for 1902, although supposedly based on a "policy of presenting full and definite financial information," did not indicate the existence of water. But the property account was increased, and no intangibles were included in the balance sheet.[111] In sum, uniform accounting standards, facilitating comparability among manufacturing concerns, were still in their infancy.

The impact of the most prestigious accounting firm of that era, Price, Waterhouse & Co., of British origin, illustrates the state of financial reporting and its evolution. Price, Waterhouse applied the same accounting standards to all of the numerous giant businesses that were its clients thus fostering a limited degree of uniformity.[112] Furthermore, by witholding its certificate of approval until the accounts were put in satisfactory order, Price, Waterhouse exerted considerable pressure and thereby additionally induced compliance. This firm emphasized the imposition of uniform principles, and it played an important part in devising accounting systems and in establishing accepted accounting procedures. When personnel from Price, Waterhouse left it to found other significant accounting firms, its ideas and policies were further diffused.

The relations between Price, Waterhouse and a key client, United States Steel, which provided exceptionally detailed financial reports, symbolize the start of a new era. In 1899, a principal constituent company of United States Steel, the Federal Steel Company, "issued one of the most complete reports published to that date."[113] Later the leader of Federal Steel, Elbert H. Gary, became the head of United States Steel. Price, Waterhouse became the auditors for United States Steel when it was organized in 1901, and Price, Waterhouse applied policies that it had used for a decade with other clients.[114] The prominence and publicity attached to United States Steel accorded its financial disclosure policy more than the ordinary share of attention.

Some giant enterprises inaugurated internal auditing in order to enhance management's ability to manage. Standard Oil was among the innovators (by 1882), and in 1902 it instituted a system of traveling auditors and examiners.[115] However, external audits remained sufficiently uncommon so that a report that a firm was subject to one could give rise to suspicions of either fraud or failure. Gradually there was an increase in the number of independent auditors and audits, but management frequently treated accountants as the servants of management. Nonetheless, the leading accountants, the heads of the major accounting firms, and the university teachers of accounting supplied some independent leadership, largely inspired by British experience.

Management in the unregulated sector of the economy, which was ultimately responsible for the quantity and quality of information made public, said little in explanation of its policies in this area. Executives of Standard Oil, explaining that an aspect of competition was to prevent the release of information, failed to supply its stockholders with a financial statement.[116] The directors of Minnesota Mining and Manufacturing concealed the financial standing of their company from their small stockholders in order to conceal it from their competitors, although those stockholders who attended the annual meeting received more information than those who did not.[117] Competition was thus used to justify many acts of omission, such as making public financial reports with so few details as to be virtually meaningless. As for acts of commission, for example, overstating profits by concealing expense items in the capital account, nothing was said.

Most railroads had inaccurate capital cost records before the Hepburn Act and to some extent after. Some deliberately padded the property account to conceal from the public and the regulatory commissions the correct relation between profits and investment.[118] Many just did not have accurate data at this time. There was no uniform or standard system of establishing the property base for rates until the Valuation Act of 1913 was implemented in the 1920s.

Financial reporting became a focal point during the Armstrong hearings, and the procedures of the giants of the life insurance industry became a cynosure. A committee of the board of directors had probed the mangement of the Equitable Life Assurance Society as part of an internal quarrel and had charged, among other things, that its accounting practices were improper. The committee report was rejected by the board; and Henry Clay Frick, chairman of the committee, Edward H. Harriman, and Cornelius N. Bliss resigned.[119] Following the Frick committee report and the Armstrong hearings, the new management of Equitable retained both Price, Waterhouse and Haskins and Sells, another outstanding accounting firm, to audit its financial affairs. They found additional details that had escaped the Frick committee.[120]

Many life insurance companies had filed false statements with the New York State Insurance Department in the years before 1905.[121] As one historian observed, "An increasingly complex investment structure and technique demanded equal complexity in accounting and bookkeeping procedure. Subterfuge and circumvention became common."[122] The report of New York Life for 1903 concealed certain pertinent facts by means of a dummy transaction. George W. Perkins, while with both J. P. Morgan and New York Life, had arranged for the sale of International Mercantile Marine stock at a high price by New York Life to J. P. Morgan at the end of 1903 and its repurchase after the start of the new year at the same price. This transaction concealed the decline in the value of the stock and thus did not appear in the annual report to the New York State Superintendent of Insurance.[123]

Charles Evans Hughes, counsel of the Armstrong committee, demanded an explanation of the behavior of New York Life. Perkins claimed: "We did it to protect our situation." Hughes retorted: "But the only situation you had to protect . . . , was the situation exigent by reason of your making your report to the superintendent of insurance."[124] Once having acted, the company had to cover its tracks.

One of the aspects of private business that businessmen defended with vigor and persistence was the traditional right to keep financial operations secret. But by World War I, financial reporting practices made deep inroads on this time-hallowed prerogative. Financial reporting became more and more uniform, and the phrase "generally accepted accounting principles" acquired substance. There were several sources of change in the morality of financial reporting. Some large-scale manufacturing enterprises already disclosed a great deal of useful financial data, using "Good business pays in the long run" as an operating principle. As management obtained superior facts and figures for its own use, it became willing to make more of its information public. The management of such concerns recognized that outsiders, such as investors, as well as insiders, had a legitimate right to know, although that right was not unbounded. These companies improved financial reporting, because they constituted a model to which external critics could effectively point.

Companies in the regulated industries, notably railroads and life insurance, during this period were compelled by government to furnish more detailed and comprehensive financial reports than before. The ripple effect converted the particularistic ethic into a universalistic ethic, and such companies set a standard of financial reporting that others could emulate and that could serve as an example for those who sought higher standards elsewhere.

Accounting was well on the road to becoming a profession. The American Association of Public Accountants had been organized in 1887, and the first certified public accounting law was passed in 1896. Accountants became more knowledgeable through experience. Furthermore the subject of accounting was now deemed worthy of being taught at leading universities. As a profession, accounting grew more self-conscious and independent. It promoted modifications in the morality of businessmen concerning financial reporting. The long-term advantages of honesty prevailed and coincided with the need of firms to impress actual and potential investors in securities.

And yet despite real advances in the morality of businessmen on this score, much more remained to be accomplished. Only with the cumulative effects of the federal income tax law in 1913, the excess profits tax in 1917, and the Securities Acts of 1933-1934 were the dominant values of the business community concerning financial reporting replaced by what had been the variant values. Legislation meant that new standards of business morality were imposed from outside on those who refused to adopt them voluntarily and, further, that the traditional defense based on anxiety about aiding competition was nullified since all firms were placed on the same plane.

The code of business morality was quite different by 1914 from what had been sanctioned in 1900, and by common consent, the difference constituted an improvement. Many veteran businessmen, especially those who had been outsiders and victims, could look back in 1914 with justifiable satisfaction on the contrast between the new and the old, although some, notably insiders, probably never did quite comprehend the extent of the change.

Part of the improvement came from within the business community. One example is the self-denial practiced by firms that shunned the patent medicine industry before the law intruded. Another is that Kuhn, Loeb rarely placed its members on the boards of its clients. In 1906 this investment banking firm publicly renounced this conflict of interest.

The announcement that the members of the firm of Kuhn, Loeb & Company had retired from all railroad directorates, had occasioned considerable comment and practically all of a favorable character. A number of newspapers have editorials to the effect that this action is likely to force other banking houses to retire from boards so that they will not be in the equivocal position of dealing with themselves on both sides of a bond transaction.[125]

But the principal force for change in business morality came from outside the business community. Businessmen must ultimately internalize the views and values of the community. Since the dominant faction resisted doing so at this juncture, an aroused public opinion wrote new concepts of business morality into law.

The morality of business can be seen in attitudes toward the law. Businessmen frequently were so confident of their righteousness that they denied the right of others to judge, contributing both to the sense of "private" business on the one hand and the opposition to government intrusion on the other.[126] Both the New York Clearing House Association and the New York Stock Exchange were conceived of by many of those who ran them as private associations, even though vested with quasi-public functions, and government supervision was rejected on those grounds. Some, however, were willing to accept government supervision to protect against errors and mistakes and to guard against the use of unregulated private power.[127] During the course of the Armstrong investigation, one life insurance executive claimed, "Those relations are confidential, sir, and I must decline to answer." Charles Evans Hughes quickly made him aware that that answer would no longer suffice: "There is nothing confidential about the insurance business now."[128]

Jacob H. Schiff, one of the most important investment bankers, asserted that something might be inadvisable and not be morally wrong. He was unwilling to accept the suggestion of Samuel Untermyer, counsel of the Pujo committee, that everything was either right or wrong.[129] Such a philosophical theme (whether all behavior, business as well as personal, was either moral or immoral, right or wrong) was not within the purview of the money trust investigation and hence not pursued further.

Similarly, Frank Knight Sturgis, a broker and a member of the New York Stock Exchange, was asked about some of the manipulative practices that were used to raise or lower prices. "I approve of transactions that pay their proper commissions and are properly transacted," he replied. "You are asking me a moral question and I an answering a stock exchange question." He contended that sometimes there is no relation between a moral question and a stock exchange question. Surprisingly, Sturgis saw short selling as a moral question and was opposed to it on this basis. Nonetheless, although a member of the board of governors of the New York Stock Exchange for many years, never had he urged that his views become the rule: "It is not part of my duty to give moral lessons to other members of the community."[130] Individual responsibility incarnate, or perhaps irresponsibility, was still dominant.

Although call loans could legally be made at the market rate, spokesmen for two banks testified that those banks never lent at above the 6 percent legally defined rate for usury. Charles W. Turner, a money broker for National City Bank, maintained: But when it [the National City Bank] has money to loan, and there is a need for money, it has always, whether from altruistic motives or not, acted in a very benevolent manner."[131]

During this period Standard Oil endeavored to comply with the letter of the law. They were made aware of the difference between the legal and the illegal by their counsel, Dodd and Elliott, and the company did a reasonably good job of complying with laws regulating interstate commerce. Dodd, Standard's chief counsel from 1881 to 1905, went even further and concerned himself not only with the interpretation of the law but also with Standard's moral obligations, and he occasionally "advocated a course of action on moral rather than legal grounds." In short, Standard Oil tried to stay within the law, but management was less adept than its attorneys in realizing that the law is dynamic and not static.[132]

The period between the elevation of Theodore Roosevelt to the presidency and the outbreak of World War I, which encompasses most of the progressive period, witnessed an unprecedented array of governmental inquiries, legislation, and administrative and judicial decisions that reformed business behavior. Conflict of interest was inhibited by the Armstrong insurance investigation and its aftermath, and railroad freight rate discrimination became a dead letter as a result of the Hepburn Act. At every hand the power of the regulators to restrain the individual, remove temptation, and delimit the range of permissible behavior was augmented, actions profoundly altering business morality. The muckraking press, and to a lesser extent the press generally, trumpeted the moral shortcomings of the nation's leading businessmen. By 1914 the business morality of the insiders and the outsiders had drawn closer together. It had not coalesced or fused but was not as divergent as before. Universalism, according to which all are judged by the same impersonal standard, pushed into the foreground, shunting particularism aside.

Self-interest was still a guide to action; as an end it was still quite acceptable. As adherence to the law improved, however, the means to that end were severely restricted. The drive to achieve was still powerful, but now the law and society set minimum rules. Deviations from them became the exception, for the law was a distillation of deeply held community values. So far as there was deviation and a self-interest, the businessman was less likely to deny the legitimacy of the law than to rationalize his behavior in some other way.

Further attempts were made to redefine what was morally acceptable during the Wilson administration and later during the administrations of Franklin D. Roosevelt. The Federal Trade Commission Act (1914) was created to restrain competition in commerce. The Clayton Antitrust Act (1914) supplemented existing antitrust legislation. These, and other laws enacted during the presidency of Woodrow Wilson, reflected demands that had lingered from the Populist Era and that did not actually affect business morality until after the close of the period under discussion. The Banking Acts of 1933 and 1935, among other things, separated commercial and investment banking. The Securities Act of 1933 and the Securities Exchange Act of 1934 provided for full and fair disclosure, which meant that investors now could anticipate annual reports of listed corporations that were both reasonably detailed and reliable.

5

THE MORAL AUDIT

Successful businessmen in large-scale enterprises are not a systematically representative sample of businessmen in general. Nevertheless, it is reasonable to suppose that the characteristics they shared were not unique to them. All occupations tend to recruit and reward those individuals who possess appropriate characteristics and thereby to develop a distinct type for each calling. Businessmen in general must have a morality, as well as talent and temperament, that will enable them or permit them to achieve success. But differences among them also exist.

Matthew Josephson, who revived and popularized the term *robber barons*, contended that "nearly all of them tended to act without those established moral principles which fixed more or less the conduct of the common people of the community."[1] This conclusion may be true, but Josephson made no effort to prove it or to prove what the morality of the commonalty was. The hypothesis that the successful businessmen of this era flouted prevailing morality more than those of a previous one can hardly be tested, and it is by no means the whole story. Furthermore, the Josephson view seems to suggest more stability in nineteenth-century moral principles than the evidence would warrant. In the dynamic society under scrutiny, the rules were necessarily precarious and undefined.

Two questions are crucial. First, did business morality change at all, in either theory or practice, between 1840 and 1914? Second, if business morality changed and, more than that, for the better, what brought about change? The toughest problem is deciding whether business became more ethical or society became more sophisticated. As to pooling by railroads and stock watering, what happened was not that businessmen reformed and stopped acting in this manner but that the practices came to have a far less insidious connotation than they had originally.

Dishonesty lessens when the rules are clarified and enforced.[2] This is one of the reasons why it is likely that business morality moved to a new plane during the three-quarters of a century with which this study is concerned. Precedent was piled upon precedent, law was piled upon law, and administrative ruling was piled upon administrative ruling. At the same time businessmen were increasingly exposed to the glare of publicity. Again and again they were called upon to make an accounting of their actions to themselves and to the public at large. As a result, in at least certain areas and circumstances, businessmen were less prone to act in 1914 as they did earlier on the five issues I have examined.

To some, however, the very fact of change in business morality is still open to question. Edmond Cahn, a professor of law, has observed, "The statistics of government reports, and our own unpleasant experiences combine to make us wonder whether any moral improvement whatever has attended the progress of industrialization."[3]

I propose several qualifications to Cahn's statement, which emphasizes evidence of deviation, not conformity. First, this study has not attempted to treat the evolution of business morality in general but instead has dealt with five specific business practices, and I have accorded only peripheral attention to other aspects of business morality. Second, the most marked transformation in the behavior of businessmen in all probability occurred in those areas in which businessmen interact with each other as insiders in conflict-of-interest situations. In such areas, the standard of honesty has risen as a concomitant of economic growth, because complex enterprises demanded it. Also, there was an extension of the time horizon, which meant that a good reputation was more valuable in the long run than a quick killing in the short run.

Certainly those who doubt the growth of morality can be safely challenged, at least on those topics I have examined here, although the historian, like the jurist, deals only with those who are caught. At the end of the period there was less conflict of interest than there had been earlier. Restraint of trade was delimited, although the structure of the American economy was not affected. Competitive tactics were modified, and certain practices virtually disappeared. Stock watering diminished in the railroads, although it continued to flourish elsewhere. Financial reporting improved, although much remained to be done. Although government left the internal affairs of large-scale enterprises quite alone until 1933, it regulated their external affairs much earlier.

To explain why there was change is another matter. Despite the mass of evidence of a descriptive nature, it is difficult to speculate confidently on the causes of historical change because so little can be known for sure about the motives of men. It is plausible to hypothesize about "the different and multiple gradations of moral standards . . . [and] the opportunities every one of us enjoys for moral creativeness."[4] As to the first matter, the evidence is abundant and clear. The second must rest on one's subjective view of the nature of cultural change. In any culture there are enormous pressures, both visible and invisible, making for stability; and yet cultures do change, in part because of the opportunities for moral creativeness. The one under examination, American business society, changed profoundly.

It is mandatory to inquire into the nature of change because of the dualism of stability and change. Self-interest was (and still is) a guide to action. Never was it the sole guide, but it was certainly a fundamental point of departure for Americans generally during the period from about 1840 to 1914. As the authors of a notable study of the ideology of businessmen observe, "There are always boundaries on legitimate means of pursuing business success. The emphasis on achievement implies a constant pressure on these boundaries of legitimacy."[5] All societies, traditional and modern, agricultural and industrial, have laws or rules that set limits on the pursuit of self-interest, and business as a subsociety is no exception. To account for moral change is indeed difficult. Some men act largely in response to something in their own nature independent of their culture.[6] It is this category that is always the most difficult to account for, and yet it is at the heart of change.

No wholly satisfactory explanation of internally derived change exists, but there are some possibilities. One reason is the range of behavior within the business culture. Each industry, indeed each firm, is a subculture with its own code, and this makes it easier for an individual to be morally creative, to be a determinant of business morality as well as a product of it, but it says nothing about why a particular individual was creative. Different social groups of businessmen have different codes, which may compete, conflict, or overlap. Codes applicable to insiders may not be applicable to outsiders.[7] If stockholders as outsiders emerge victorious in a struggle for control with insiders, they might impose new ethical standards.

The possibility of internal change arising from individual creativity was limited by competition. It was difficult to eliminate bad actors and to unite an entire industry for self-regulation because tactics commonly condemned as immoral did win competitive advantages.[8] Much of self-regulation either by a businessman or in conjunction with his fellows is not based on a self-sacrificing internalization of the views of the community but rather on a more selfish desire to remain one step ahead of the law. Businessmen have typically pursued their self-interest; some ways are approved, while others are not.

Internal changes in business morality did occur regarding conflict of interest. One decisive turn of events, the Burlington's revolution of 1875, was in no way related to the passage of new laws. Much more to the point was anxiety on the part of insiders lest revelations about conflict of interest threaten investment by the public.[9] But elements of inconsistency surely lingered. Because of the support of Moses Taylor, a New York banker and investor, James F. Joy, although ousted from the presidency of the Burlington, retained the presidency of the Michigan Central.[10] On the other hand, Charles Elliott Perkins, an associate of Forbes, from the early 1860s to the late 1870s bought land with a clear conscience, using his inside information about the Burlington's plans. James J. Hill of the Great Northern dealt differently with his stockholders with regard to the Mesabi iron-ore lands during the early twentieth century; he refrained from conflict-of-interest behavior and opposed it in others. These, however, were not the same times nor was the same man involved.[11] In general, legislation was of little consequence in the later diminution of conflict of interest, although legislation affecting the life insurance industry, passed in the aftermath of the Armstrong investigation, represents a notable exception. The main reason for change as to conflict of interest was the increase in the size and financial strength of enterprises that adopted their own rules. The Louisville & Nashville, for example, imposed such a rule in 1876 although the railroad had been in operation for more than two decades.[12] This reason was coupled with the pragmatic fact that honest management, in the long run, had perceptible advantages in the capital market. Perkins uttered a cry from the heart: "We railroad men had bad [enough] reputations to stagger under before, but the Boston management [of the Burlington] had been beyond suspicion. Now the public thinks we are all thieves!"[13] Such evidence suggests that Forbes and those who sided with him during the revolution of 1875 were not exclusively concerned with abstract notions of right and wrong. They were concerned with a kind of fiduciary relationship established with their investors; to act as both buyer and seller was to jeopardize that relationship.

"As the old adage 'honesty is the best policy' indicates," according to Thomas Cochran, a leading business historian, "the immediate basis of the general sanction against business dishonesty was business efficiency rather than abstract morality."[14] There was a shift in the so-called permanent or quasi-public enterprises toward the long-term view on the maximization of profits and on the belief that good business pays in the long run. The pursuit of short-term self-interest often means not only the moral but also the economic long-term disadvantage.[15]

For the most part the pressures for change in business morality came from outside. Most men do not have such finely tuned consciences that they will act against what they perceive as their own self-interest. Defenders of business argued for reliance on good men rather than good laws, while critics of business insisted that business immorality required action by government.[16]

The opportunities for business transgression were lessened during the period under study. The separation of the stock register from the stock transfer agent prevented management from converting the proceeds of the sale of securities to its own purpose. As the financial strength of railroads increased, they used outside rather than inside construction companies. Change in business morality occurred quite frequently because society, instigated largely by aggrieved customers, colleagues, and competitors, adopted the contention of the critics.

Internalization can frequently be delayed and change retarded in business morality by obstacles that arise from self-interest. There has been less change in business morality concerning restraint of trade than in the other business practices under discussion. An examination of restraint of trade necessitates the conclusion that, to the extent that there has been any change at all, it has been derived from the Sherman Antitrust Act as amended and as interpreted by the courts; however, there are numerous examples of breaches of the antitrust law, which itself constitutes a minimum standard of morality. The price conspiracy case in the electrical machinery industry in 1961 exemplifies behavior that participants must have known involved illegal action. This is an illustration in which the commonly accepted business behavior was, and still is, below the standard prescribed by the law.

The forces for the reform of competitive tactics were augmented by businessmen. Virtually no businessman could, for example, compete without accepting rebates if his competitors avidly sought them, but he could and did mobilize in order to secure the sanction of law. "From every standpoint," wrote Mark Sullivan, "it was to the advantage of the better class among these to have the dangerous and dishonest practices of their unscrupulous competitors curbed." The reform movement was intricately criss-crossed with motives entertained by various groups of businessmen.[17] As a result of the attack on big business, many businessmen gradually substituted the code of the outsiders for that of the insiders in evaluating themselves and their peers. Some chose not to sell patent medicine; others declined to avail themselves of the benefits of freight rate discrimination, and still others campaigned actively against it. Management continued to decide what a shareholder might know about his company, but some managements provided more information in their financial reports than either the law or custom required. As an illustration that change was by no means linear, the Louisville & Nashville furnished better financial reports prior to 1875 under Albert Fink than it did in the early 1880s under less able and less moral management.[18] Certainly the explanation for specific changes in business morality is not typically either internal or external but rather both.

The motives of men are obscure indeed, and Thomas C. Cochran, one of the ablest students of American business society, expressed his view as a reasoned act of faith: "There is no theoretical reason why important innovations in role behavior could not arise from inner-conditioning independently of all immediate exogenous factors. It is merely the bias of my historical observation that I think such instances rare."[19] The evidence presented here tends to support this conclusion that change in business morality was preponderantly derived from external rather than internal sources.

The process of external change was by no means simple. The key element in the drive for external change in business morality, at least in terms of initiating the process, was the victim. The historical mechanism thereafter was the expansion of the victim's moral outrage by publicity and the activities of crusaders to make it the public conscience. Government investigations hastened the crystallization of public and business opinion concerning alleged good or evil methods or results in business.[20] Small wonder that a member of the Memphis Merchants' Exchange remarked: "If businessmen cannot be honest from principle, let them be so through fear of public condemnation."[21] Once the public conscience was successfully aroused, then the perpetrator of the deed to which the public voiced objection was placed on the defensive. Eventually the aid of government as the agent of society was invoked and appropriate legislation was enacted. The provisions of legislation and decisions interpreting the law define the new morality, identifying the permitted and prohibited actions.

Change results when a sufficiently large and influential segment of the population becomes persuaded that new rules are necessary and when acceptance of the new rules becomes virtually universal. It is occasionally not enough to have a bare majority pass a law, however. Changing business morality requires something more than a legislative enactment. There must also be internalization of the rule by the individual, which is a gradual and intermittent process. If this does not materialize, then the violations may become endemic, and the rule will fail to accomplish its purpose.

What determines whether the new rules on paper become new rules in behavior? The answer to this crucial questions is sanctions. All moral codes are violated to some extent, and the strength of the sanctions determines the link between the code and social action. What punishments are inflicted by the individual upon himself (guilt) or by society (ostracism, fines, or prison) if an individual transgresses? Is the way of the transgressor hard? Certain business behavior, such as railroad rebates, ceased to be a matter of social concern, because the sanctions became strong and well established. On the other hand, restraint of trade violations by giant enterprises are still so frequent (although in varied forms) that the moral objective of the rules is not fully translated into behavior in this area. Nevertheless, while in the short run the sanctions of the insiders may prevail, in the long run those of the outsiders are more likely to prevail.[22]

Power and morality are inseparable. Considerations of the evolution of business morality without reference to the restructuring of economic power are invalid. The inequality of power in the market place that came to the fore with the rise of the giant enterprise created implications of business morality because of the failure of morality to be commensurate with power. As its historian observed, the possession of power by an enterprise, such as the Southern Pacific, demands "a sense of morality more than ordinarily acute."[23]

Standard Oil failed to realize that power confers responsibility and that practices that might be acceptable in a small firm were regarded as unfair if applied by a dominant firm.[24] This was indeed the course of events; the largest enterprises attracted the greatest notoriety. A century ago prices were set by the interaction of substantially equal buyers and sellers, and each transaction was a bargain struck by buyer and seller. But large buyers and large sellers possessed an enormous advantage as compared with other and less fortunate competitors. It was the inequality of power, and not the presumed immorality of price discrimination, that caused the demand for a one-price policy. For that matter, bargaining was replaced by a one-price policy in retailing for purely practical reasons that had nothing to do with morality.

The business leadership of each generation is something other than an exact replica of the one that preceded it and has somewhat varying notions of right and wrong: "In general, major changes in sanctions require the span of a generation or more. They have to wait for men, conditioned to some degree by the new situations, to develop new conceptions of their proper social role."[25] The laws violated by businessmen are recent and lack a firm foundation in public ethics, and sometimes the law is in conflict with business ethics. Therefore the public (and the businessmen) do not regard them in the same light as burglary.[26] A violation of the legal code is not necessarily a violation of the business code. Businessmen do not conceive of themselves as criminals when they violate the law. The most persistent and relevant illustration of this idea is the antitrust laws. Businessmen do not regard those involved in such actions as having lost prestige.[27]

John D. Rockefeller, born in 1839, was a businessman of national significance by the time he was forty and by about the turn of the century was semiretired. In contrast, businessmen who were active in 1900 were schooled at a time when large-scale enterprises already existed and there had already been a generation of moral concern as a reaction. The external world affects change in business morality and, unless one posits a world in which there was less dynamism in American business society than actually existed, one could hardly expect that a business leader of the middle of the nineteenth century could have the identical morality as one half a century later.

The normative business morality of the historically noteworthy titans I have cited was in a state of flux in the span of the seventy-five years during which America became the world's leading producer, although more decisively for some business practices than for others. Men in general, and goal-oriented businessmen in particular, are incapable of a rapid rate of self-improvement. The tendency to test the limits of moral and legal authority is all but universal. Therefore, the prime impetus for raising the standard of business morality came from the disaffected. Self-interest was as much as ever a guide to action for the businessman, who continued to define it in terms of achievement, but the choice of weapons was narrowed. All was never fair in business, although society, as it acquired greater understanding, in some instances came to accept what it had opposed earlier. Still, more became unfair with each passing generation. The ends remained constant but the means dramatically changed.

NOTES

CHAPTER 1

1. John Maurice Clark, *The Ethical Basis of Human Freedom* (New York: Kazanjian Foundation Lectures, 1955), p. 15.
2. Aldous Huxley, *Ends and Means* (New York: Harpers, 1937), p. 20.
3. Arthur M. Schlesinger, Jr., *The Age of Jackson* (Boston: Little, Brown, 1946), p. 510.
4. Frank Chapman Sharp and Philip G. Fox, *Business Ethics* (New York: Appleton-Century, 1937), p. 124.
5. Arthur H. Cole, *Business Enterprise in Its Social Setting* (Cambridge, Mass.: Harvard University Press, 1959), p. 129.

CHAPTER 2

1. Donald McConnell, *Economic Virtues in the United States* (New York, 1930), p. 59.
2. Thomas C. Cochran, *Railroad Leaders, 1845-1890* (Cambridge, Mass.: Harvard University Press, 1953), p. 124.
3. Arthur Twining Hadley, *Standards of Public Morality* (New York: Macmillan, 1907), pp. 80-81.
4. Edward Chase Kirkland, *Men, Cities and Transportation* (Cambridge, Mass.: Harvard University Press, 1948), 1:260-66; Alfred D. Chandler, Jr., *Henry Varnum Poor* (Cambridge, Mass.: Harvard University Press, 1956), p. 133.
5. Chandler, *Henry Varnum Poor*, p. 133.
6. Paul Wallace Gates, *The Illinois Central Railroad and Its Coloniza-

tion Work (Cambridge, Mass.: Harvard University Press, 1934), p. 166.

7. Chandler, *Henry Varnum Poor*, p. 113.

8. J. M. Forbes to G. Ashburner, January 19, 1857 (italics Forbes), cited in Sarah Forbes Hughes, ed., *Letters and Recollections of John Murray Forbes* (Boston: Houghton Mifflin, 1900), 1:162–63.

9. Jules I. Bogen, *The Anthracite Railroads* (New York: Ronald Press, 1927), p. 87 citing George D. Phelps, *Railroad Mismanagement, The Dangers of Exposing It and the Difficulty in Correcting It Illustrated*; Daniel Hodas, *The Business Career of Moses Taylor* (New York: New York University Press, 1976), pp. 96–98 citing George Phelps, *History of the Investigation of the D.L.&W.*, pp. 23–24, 46, 68 and George D. Phelps, *Railroad Mismanagement: The Dangers of Exposing It and the Difficulty in Correcting It Illustrated*, p. 4.

10. Edward Harold Mott, *Between the Ocean and the Lakes* (New York: John S. Collins, 1899), p. 123.

11. George Rogers Taylor, *The Transportation Revolution* (New York: Rinehart, 1951), p. 101; Cochran, *Railroad Leaders*, p. 116.

12. Irene D. Neu, *Erastus Corning* (Ithaca: Cornell University Press, 1960), pp. 168–69.

13. Ibid., pp. 169–71; Edward Hungerford, *Men and Iron* (New York: Crowell, 1938), p. 94; Alvin F. Harlow, *The Road of the Century* (New York: Creative Age Press, 1947), p. 83.

14. Hungerford, *Men and Iron*, p. 189; *New York Tribune*, 1863, cited in Harlow, *Road of the Century*, p. 111.

15. New York State Legislature, Assembly, *Proceedings of the Special Committee on Railroads, Appointed under a Resolution of the Assembly, February 23, 1879, to Investigate Alleged Abuses in the Management of Railroads Chartered by the State of New York, A. B. Hepburn, Chairman* (New York: 1879), 2:1109, 1314; 5:3769 (hereafter cited as Hepburn).

16. Wheaton J. Lane, *Commodore Vanderbilt* (New York: Knopf, 1942), p. 231 citing Vanderbilt testimony, *Jenks v. The New York Central Railroad Company* as reported in the *New York Herald*, January 20, 1869; p. 234.

17. Cochran, *Railroad Leaders*, pp. 113–15; Henry Greenleaf Pearson, *An American Railroad Builder* (Boston: Houghton Mifflin, 1911), pp. 163–78; Richard C. Overton, *Burlington Route* (New York: Knopf, 1965), pp. 122–35; Thomas C. Cochran, "Henry Villard: Entrepreneur," in Edward N. Saveth, ed., *Understanding the American Past* (Boston: Little, Brown, 1954), pp. 372–74.

18. J. M. Forbes to a director of the C.B.&Q., August 7, 1873, cited in Pearson, *American Railroad Builder*, p. 165.

19. Ibid., July 13, 1873, cited in Pearson, *American Railroad Builder*, p. 163.

20. Ibid., November 9, 1873, cited in Pearson, *American Railroad Builder*, p. 170.

21. J. M. Forbes to James F. Joy, May 14, 1875 (italics Forbes), cited in Cochran, *Railroad Leaders*, p. 335.

22. Cochran, "Henry Villard: Entrepreneur," pp. 372–74.

23. J. M. Forbes to J. C. Green, June 16, 1873, cited in Overton, *Burlington Route*, p. 132.

24. J. Brooks, director, C.B.&Q. and of River Roads, to J. Joy, former director, C.B.&Q. and director of River Roads, March 11, 1875, cited in Cochran, *Railroad Leaders*, p. 114.

25. J. N. Denison, director, C.B.&Q., to Erastus Corning, Jr., March 11, 1875, cited in Ibid., pp. 308–09.

26. Overton, *Burlington Route*, pp. 139, 147, 154–55.

27. Hughes, *John Murray Forbes*, 2:215.

28. J. M. Forbes to J. Sanborn, unidentified, June 10, 1879, cited in Cochran, *Railroad Leaders*, p. 336.

29. W. H. Osborn, president, Illinois Central, to F. Haven, ex-director, March 30, 1863, cited in Cochran, *Railroad Leaders*, p. 110.

30. G. W. Cass, Jr., President, Northern Pacific, to J. Ainsworth, director, May 15, 1873, ibid.

31. Maury Klein, *History of the Louisville & Nashville Railroad* (New York: Macmillan, 1972), p. 230.

32. Hepburn, 2:1524–26.

33. Cochran, *Railroad Leaders*, p. 117.

34. W. H. Osborn, president, Illinois Central, to J. Douglas, solicitor, Illinois Central, March 28, 1865, ibid., p. 424.

35. J. M. Forbes, director, C.B.&Q., to J. C. Green, C.B.&Q., June 20, 1873, ibid., p. 334.

36. Hepburn, 3:2451, 2485.

37. Louis C. Hunter, *Studies in the Economic History of the Ohio Valley*, Smith College Studies in History, Volume 19 (Northampton: Smith College, 1933–1934), pp. 96–97, 99, 122; Louis C. Hunter, *Steamboats on the Western Rivers* (Cambridge, Mass.: Harvard University Press, 1949), pp. 309, 516.

38. Lane, *Commodore Vanderbilt*, pp. 61–62.

39. William Z. Ripley, *Railroads: Finance and Organization* (New York: Longmans, Green, 1920), p. 582.

40. Hunter, *Studies in the Economic History of the Ohio Valley* p. 88.

41. Hungerford, *Men and Iron*, pp. 109–10.

42. Balthasar Henry Meyer, ed., *History of Transportation in the United States before 1860* (Washington, D.C.: Carnegie Institution, 1917), p. 569.

43. J. M. Forbes, president, Michigan Central, to J. Brooks, cited in Cochran, *Railroad Leaders*, p. 172.

44. Hepburn, 1:339, 489; 4:3020, 3035; 5:3974.

45. Ibid., 6:139.

46. David R. Gilchrist, "Albert Fink and the Pooling System," *Business History Review* 34 (Spring 1960): 33 citing *First Annual Report on the Internal Commerce of the United States*, House Exec. Doc. 44th Cong., 2d sess., no. 45, pt. 2, June 30, 1887 appendix, pp. 1–16, p. 12, A. Fink to J. Nimmo, Jr., May 1, 1876; Hepburn, 1:532.

47. Hepburn, 5:3979, 3981–82.

48. Albro Martin, "The Troubled Subject of Railroad Regulation —A Reappraisal," *Journal of American History* 61 (September, 1974):351–52.

49. Allan Nevins, *A Study in Power* (New York: Scribner's, 1953), 1:335; Cochran, *Railroad Leaders*, p. 171; Lee Benson, *Merchants, Farmers, & Railroads* (Cambridge, Mass.: Harvard University Press, 1955), p. 233.

50. Hepburn, 1:770.

51. Benson, *Merchants, Farmers, & Railroads*, p. 233.

52. Hunter, *Studies in the Economic History of the Ohio Valley*, pp. 51, 53–56, 123–24.

53. Samuel Eliot Morison, *The Ropemakers of Plymouth* (Boston: Houghton Mifflin, 1950), pp. 32, 44–45; Allan Nevins, *Abran S. Hewitt* (New York: Harpers, 1935), p. 109; Hunter, *Studies in the Economic History of the Ohio Valley*, p. 78; Thomas C. Cochran and William Miller, *The Age of Enterprise* (New York: Macmillan, 1942), p. 6.

54. Ralph W. Hidy and Muriel Hidy, *Pioneering in Big Business* (New York: Harpers, 1955), p. 33.

55. Harold F. Williamson and Arnold R. Daum, *The Age of Illumination* (Evanston, Ill.: Northwestern University Press, 1959), pp. 352, 549.

56. Kirkland, *Men, Cities and Transportation*, 1:354, quoting *Proceedings of the Convention of the Northern Lines of Railway*, held at Boston, in December 1850, p. 23.

57. Meyer, *Transportation in the United States*, p. 567, citing *Proceedings of the Convention of the Northern Lines of Railway*, 1851, p. 29.

58. Benson, *Merchants, Farmers, & Railroads*, pp. 71–72.

59. Hepburn, 1:123, 134, 140–44, 162, 223, 343–51, 414.

60. Ibid., pp. 84, 167, 265.

61. Hidy and Hidy, *Pioneering in Big Business*, pp. 7, 32.

62. Williamson and Daum, *Age of Illumination*, pp. 196, 301.

63. Nevins, *Study in Power*, 1:64.

64. Hidy and Hidy, *Pioneering in Big Business*, pp. 7, 32; Williamson and Daum, *Age of Illumination*, p. 353.

65. Nevins, *Study in Power*, 2:40; Hidy and Hidy, *Pioneering in Big Business*, p. 34.

66. Hidy and Hidy, *Pioneering in Big Business*, p. 34.

67. Ibid.; Nevins, *Study in Power*, 1:263.

68. Nevins, *Study in Power*, 1:66.

69. Ibid., p. 68, citing Pennsylvania Senate Inquiry, pp. 7ff.

70. Chester McArthur Destler, "The Standard Oil, Child of the Erie Ring, 1868–1872,"*Mississippi Valley Historical Review*, 33 (June 1946):89–114.

71. Nevins, *Study in Power, 1:70, 93*–94, 113–14, quoting William O. Inglis, *Conversations with Rockefeller*, 1917, Rockefeller Papers.

72. Ibid., p. 121.

73. Letter to the *Cleveland Herald*, March 6, 1872, ibid., p. 123.

74. Hidy and Hidy, *Pioneering in Big Business*, p. 16.

75. Ibid.; Nevins, *Study in Power*, 1:114, 259; Williamson and Daum, *Age of Illumination*, p. 350.

76. J. D. Rockefeller to L. S. Rockefeller, March 15, 1872, cited in Nevins, *Study in Power*, 1:114–15.

77. "The testimony taken before the [Hepburn] committee has never been printed in the series of collected docs. [of New York State]. An edition of 100 copies was printed during the sessions of the committee for its use and the use of counsel and prominent r.r. officers." *See* Adelaide R. Hasse, *Index to Documents of the State of New York* (Washington, D.C.: Carnegie Institution, 1907), p. 467.

78. Hepburn, 1:414, 491–92, 495, 505; 4:2851; 5:3632.

79. Ibid., 1:280, 451; 3:2738–39; 4:2825, 2855.

80. Ibid., 1:40–44.

81. Benson, *Merchants, Farmers, & Railroads*, p. 129, quoting *Evening Post*, June 19, 1879.

82. Hepburn, 1:453.

83. Stuart Daggett, *Chapters on the History of the Southern Pacific* (New York: Ronald Press, 1922), p. 239.

84. Hepburn, 1:301.

85. Ibid., 3:2617–18, 2654–55, 2668.

86. Albro Martin, *James J. Hill and the Opening of the Northwest* (New York: Oxford University Press, 1976), p. 55.

87. John P. Davis, *The Union Pacific Railway* (Chicago: S. G. Griggs, 1894), p. 198.

88. Kirkland, *Men, Cities and Transportation*, 2:318–19.

89. Harry H. Pierce, *Railroads of New York* (Cambridge, Mass.: Harvard University Press, 1953), p. 80; Neu, *Erastus Corning*, p. 163; Frank Walker Stevens, *The Beginnings of the New York Central Railroad* (New York: Putnam, 1926), pp. 350, 358–59, 364–71, 378–79.

90. Hungerford, *Men and Iron*, p. 216.

91. Chandler, *Henry Varnum Poor*, pp. 135–36; Neu, *Erastus Corning*, pp. 165–66, citing *New York Times*, April 16, 1853; *American Railroad Journal* 9 (April 23, 1853):266, 10 (May 27, 1854):330–31; *New York Tribune*, July 8, 1853.

92. Stevens, *New York Central Railroad*, pp. 382–83.

93. Harlow, *Road of the Century*, p. 193; Benson, *Merchants, Farmers, & Railroads*, p. 136; Hepburn, 2:1116.

94. Hungerford, *Men and Iron*, p. 218; Benson, *Merchants, Farmers, & Railroads*, pp. 77, 137.

95. Benson, *Merchants, Farmers, & Railroads*, p. 129.

96. Hepburn, 1:53.

97. Lane, *Commodore Vanderbilt*, pp. 233–34.

98. Hepburn, 2:1395, 1637.

99. Nevins, *Abram S. Hewitt*, pp. 109–10.

100. Kirkland, *Men, Cities and Transportation*, 2:335.

101. Chandler, *Henry Varnum Poor*, pp. 137–40, 141.

102. Mott, *Between the Ocean and the Lakes*, p. 116.

103. J. M. Forbes, director, C.B.&.Q., to F. Tyson, auditor, C.B.&.Q., January 4, 1876, quoted in Cochran, *Railroad Leaders*, p. 335.

104. Mott, *Between the Ocean and the Lakes*, p. 206.

105. Hepburn, 2:1396.

106. Ibid., 5:3902, 3998; Benson, *Merchants, Farmers, & Railroads*, p. 5.

107. Edward Hungerford, *Men of Erie* (New York: Random House, 1946), p. 178; Mott, *Between the Ocean and the Lakes*, pp. 223–37; Stuart Daggett, *Railroad Reorganization* (Boston: Houghton Mifflin, 1908), p. 37, citing *Railroad Gazette*, 6 (1874):100.

108. Julius Grodinsky, *Jay Gould* (Philadelphia: University of Pennsylvania Press, 1957), p. 191, citing *New York Tribune*, June 18, 1878.

109. Harold F. Williamson, *Edward Atkinson* (Boston: Old Corner Book Store, 1934), p. 39.

110. E. Atkinson to W. D. Crane, February 14, 1873, Ibid.

111. Benson, *Merchants, Farmers, & Railroads*, pp. 142–44.

112. John Henry Devereux, general manager, Lake Shore and Michigan

Southern, to Horace Clark, June 10, 1871, cited in Cochran, *Railroad Leaders*, p. 312.

113. Ibid., pp. 23, 124, 125.

114. Mott, *Between the Ocean and the Lakes*, p. 253.

115. Charles Francis Adams, Jr., and Henry Adams, *Chapters of Erie* (New York: Holt, 1886), p. 95; Edward Chase Kirkland, *Charles Francis Adams, Jr., 1835–1915* (Cambridge, Mass.: Harvard University Press, 1965), offers considerable insight into this ambivalent figure.

116. Hepburn, 5:3972.

117. Ibid., 2:1452, 1480; 6:122.

CHAPTER 3

1. Richard C. Overton, *Gulf to Rockies* (Austin, Tex.: University of Texas Press, 1953), pp. 102, 106, 107, 125, 128.

2. *Railway Gazette*, December 19, 1913, pp 1197–98.

3. Arthur Pound and Samuel Taylor Moore, eds., *More They Told Barron* (New York: Harpers, 1931), p. 132.

4. N. P. Eells to W. B. Crittenden, May 12, 1894, cited in Harold F. Williamson and Kenneth H. Myers, *Designed for Digging* (Evanston, Ill.: Northwestern University Press, 1955), p. 47.

5. Allan Nevins, *Study in Power* (New York: Scribner's, 1953), 1:389, 397–98; 2:41. Ralph W. Hidy and Muriel E. Hidy, *Pioneering in Big Business* (New York: Harpers, 1955), p. 65.

6. Charles M. Higgins to Allan Nevins, January 13, 17, 1937, cited in Nevins, *Study in Power*, 2:17–18.

7. Donald McConnell, *Economic Virtues in the United States* (New York, 1930), p. 95; George Harvey, *Henry Clay Frick* (New York: Scribner's, 1928), pp. 221–27, 237; James Howard Bridge, *The Inside History of the Carnegie Steel Company* (New York: Aldine, 1903), pp. 298–99.

8. Joseph Frazier Wall, *Andrew Carnegie* (New York: Oxford University Press, 1970), pp. 732–60.

9. Thomas C. Cochran, *Railroad Leaders, 1845–1890* (Cambridge, Mass.: Harvard University Press, 1953), p. 225.

10. Milton H. Smith to the directors of the Louisville & Nashville Railroad Company, September 23, 1886, cited in Maury Klein, *History of the Louis & Nashville Railroad* (New York: Macmillan, 1972), p. 233.

11. William Taussig, *Ethics of Railway Management* (St Louis: R. P. Studley, 1898), pp. 13–14.

12. T. Jefferson Coolidge, *Autobiography* (Boston: Houghton Mifflin,

1923), p. 88; James Marshall, *Santa Fe* (New York: Random House, 1945), p. 168; Edward C. Kirkland, *Industry Comes of Age* (New York: Holt, Rinehart and Winston, 1961), p. 227.

13. Atchinson, Topeka & Santa Fe, *Annual Report* (1888), p. 17.

14. G. M. Dodge to T. F. Pearsall, director, Denver, Texas and Gulf, April 2, 1887, cited in Overton, *Gulf to Rockies* p. 160.

15. Grenville M. Dodge to Morgan Jones, May 15, 1898, ibid., pp. 359–60.

16. Frederick Billings, president, Northern Pacific, to James B. Power, land commissioner, October 27, 1880, cited in Cochran, *Railroad Leaders*, p. 257.

17. Thomas Fletcher Oakes, vice-president, Northern Pacific, to J. N. Dolph, vice-president, Oregon Railway & Navigation, September 11, 1882, ibid., p. 415.

18. Henry Villard, president, Northern Pacific, to Charles Fairchild, Baring Bros., April 2, 1883, ibid., pp. 112, 483.

19. Henry Villard, president, Northern Pacific, to "Dear Cousin," July 11, 1883, ibid., pp. 484–85.

20. Albro Martin, *James J. Hill and the Opening of the Northwest* (New York: Oxford University Press, 1976), pp. 440–41.

21. James C. Clarke, president, Illinois Central, to Stuyvesant Fish, vice-president, November 18, 1885, cited in Cochran, *Railroad Leaders*, pp. 300–01.

22. Frederick J. Kimball, vice-president, Norfolk & Western, to Henry Fink, 2nd vice-president, June 16, 1881, ibid., p. 370.

23. Frederick J. Kimball, president, Norfolk & Western, to Everett Gray, director, February 19, 1886, ibid., p. 373.

24. John Murray Forbes, president, C.B.&Q., to Lucius Tuckerman, Chicago, Rock Island & Pacific, February 14, 1880, ibid., p. 338.

25. Ibid., pp. 124, 338. Arthur H. Cole, *Business Enterprise in Its Social Setting* (Cambridge, Mass.: Harvard University Press, 1959), p. 241, presents an unblemished view.

26. C. E. Perkins to A. E. Touzalin, May 2, 1881, cited in Overton, *Gulf to Rockies*, p. 101.

27. Charles Elliott Perkins, president, C.B.& Q., to Thomas J. Potter, vice-president, August 13, 1885, cited in Cochran, *Railroad Leaders*, p. 117.

28. Charles Elliott Perkins, president, C.B.& Q., to John Murray Forbes, chairman, July 15, 1883, ibid., p. 436.

29. U.S., Industrial Commission, *Reports of the Industrial Commission*, 19 vols. (Washington D.C.: Government Printing Office, 1900–02) 1:974.

30. Ibid., 13:279–71.

31. Ibid., p. 449.

32. Harold Passer, *The Electrical Manufacturers* (Cambridge, Mass.: Harvard University Press, 1953), p. 291.

33. U.S., Industrial Commission, 1:1175.

34. Ibid., 4:103, 152, 215.

35. David T. Gilchrist, "Albert Fink and the Pooling System," *Business History Review* 34 (Spring 1960): 47.

36. Ibid., p. 48.

37. U.S., Industrial Commission, 4:157, 643.

38. Ibid., p. 648; Gilchrist, "Fink and the Pooling System," p. 47.

39. U.S., Industrial Commission, 4:14, 62, 100, 236, 280, 361, 391, 474, 495, 539, 678.

40. Henry Brockholst Ledyard, president, Michigan Central, to J. Clements, unidentified, November 21, 1888, cited in Cochran, *Railroad Leaders*, pp. 404–05.

41. Charles Elliott Perkins, president, C.B.&Q., to William W. Baldwin, land commissioner, December 7, 1886, ibid., pp. 172, 445.

42. Henry Brockholst Ledyard, president, Michigan Central, to Rev. D. M. Cooper, March 5, 1889, ibid., p. 165.

43. George Henry Watrous, president, New York, New Haven & Hartford, to Chauncey M. Depew, 2nd vice-president, New York Central & Hudson River, December 13, 1884, ibid., p. 166.

44. George Henry Watrous, president, New York, New Haven & Hartford, to Charles Rockwell, General Freight Agent, July 1, 1885, ibid., p. 499.

45. Julius Grodinsky, *Jay Gould* (Philadelphia: University of Pennsylvania Press, 1957), p. 565. No evidence is cited for this, however.

46. U.S., Industrial Commission, 13:474; Harold Williamson, *Winchester* (Washington, D.C.: Combat Forces Press, 1952), p. 121.

47. John R. Houston, president and agent of the Hartford Carpet Company to his directorate, Hartford Carpet Company, Minutes of the Directors' and Stockholders' meeting, February 19, 1892, cited in John S. Ewing and Nancy P. Norton, *Broadlooms and Businessmen* (Cambridge, Mass.: Harvard University Press, 1955), p. 164.

48. Samuel Eliot Morison, *The Ropemakers of Plymouth* (Boston: Houghton Mifflin, 1950), pp. 77–85.

49. U.S., Industrial Commission, 13:126, 164.

50. Charles Elliott Perkins, president, C.B.&Q., to William W. Baldwin, land commissioner, December 7, 1886, cited in Cochran, *Railroad Leaders*, p. 445.

51. U.S., Industrial Commission, 1:112, 118, 158.

52. Ibid., p. 159. See also ibid., pp. 237, 272–73; 13:603, 606; Harold F. Williamson and Arnold R. Daum, *The Age of Illumination* (Evanston, Ill.: Northwestern University Press, 1959), p. 710, citing *State ex rel* v. *Standard Oil Company*, 49 Ohio St. 137 (1892), 185–86.

53. Josesph A. Schumpeter, *Business Cycles* (New York: McGraw-Hill, 1939), 1:294n.

54. U.S., Industrial Commission, 1:637, 1190; 19:351–54.

55. Ibid., 4:132, 133, 168, 273, 675, 767; 19:349, 350.

56. Ibid., 4:594, 625.

57. Henry Brockholst Ledyard, president, Michigan Central, to W. K. Muir, president, Eureka Iron & Steel Works, September 9, 1885, cited in Cochran, *Railroad Leaders*, p. 393.

58. George Henry Watrous, president, New York, New Haven & Hartford, to William D. Bishop, director and ex-president, March 12, 1886, ibid., pp. 499–500.

59. Henry Brockholst Ledyard, president, Michigan Central, to William H. Perry, General Eastern Freight agent, June 4, 1883, ibid., p. 386.

60. Frederick J. Kimball, vice-president, Norfolk & Western, to E. T. Steel, president, Southwest Virginia Improvement Company, December 9, 1882, ibid., p. 371.

61. James C. Clarke, president, Illinois Central, to Stephen Little, general auditor, Erie, September 18, 1885, ibid., p. 300.

62. Hidy and Hidy, *Pioneering in Big Business*, pp. 31, 97.

63. U.S., Industrial Commission, 4:635.

64. U.S., Industrial Commission, *Final Report of the Industrial Commission* (Washington, D.C.: Government Printing Office, 1902), 19:659, supplementary statement of Mr. Phillips (Minority Report) quoting unpublished stenographic reports of testimony by railroad officials before the Interstate Commerce Commission.

65. Taussig, *Ethics of Railway Management*, p. 8.

66. Stuart Daggett, *Chapters on the History of the Southern Pacific* (New York: Ronald Press, 1922), p. 240.

67. U.S., Industrial Commission, 4:561.

68. Ibid., 1:1190.

69. Ibid., 1:1190; 4:279–81, 471.

70. Ibid., 4:238, 286.

71. Ibid., p. 684.

72. Ibid., 1:579; 4:257.

73. Ibid., 1:787.

74. Ibid., p. 110.

75. Ibid., pp. 110, 112–13.

76. Ibid., 9:748.

77. Ibid., 4:353–54.

78. Ibid., p. 152; 19:323, 344.

79. Ibid., 13:470; 14:350.

80. J. Owen Stalson, *Marketing Life Insurance* (Cambridge, Mass: Harvard University Press, 1942), p. 535.

81. Harris Proschansky, "The National Association of Life Underwriters" (Ph.D. dis., New York University, 1954), p. 123, citing *Weekly Statement*, 18, re 10, October 11, 1893, p. 83.

82. Ibid., pp. 123–24.

83. John A. Garraty, *Right-Hand Man* (New York: Harpers [1960]), pp. 48–49.

84. Harold F. Williamson and Orange A. Smalley, *Northwestern Mutual Life* (Evanston, Ill.: Northwestern University Press, 1957), p. 111.

85. Proschansky, "National Association of Life Underwriters," p. 149; Stalson, *Marketing Life Insurance*, p. 535.

86. U.S., Industrial Commission, 1:58–59; 13:374, 392, 322.

87. Boris Emmet and John Jeuck, *Catalogues and Counters* (Chicago: University of Chicago Press, 1950), p. 728, n. 34.

88. Ibid., pp. 69–70, citing statement of a former catalog editor based on his own experience.

89. Ibid., p. 110.

90. U.S., Industrial Commission, 1:128.

91. Williamson and Smalley, *Northwestern Mutual Life*, p. 110.

92. Ralph M. Hower, *The History of an Advertising Agency* (Cambridge, Mass.: Harvard University Press, 1949), pp. 91–92.

93. Frank Presbrey, *The History and Development of Advertising* (Garden City: Doubleday, Doran, 1929), pp. 531–32; Edward Bok, *The Americanization of Edward Bok* (New York: Scribner's 1924), p. 340; Hower, *History of an Advertising Agency*, pp. 90, 602, n. 49.

94. Passer, *Electrical Manufacturers*, pp. 318–19, citing *Electrical World*, 25 (May 25, 1895): 603.

95. Williamson, *Winchester*, pp. 151–52.

96. Paul Babcock to John D. Rockefeller, undated, 1888, cited in Hidy and Hidy, *Pioneering in Big Business*, p. 214.

97. U.S., Industrial Commission, 1:136.

98. Ibid., pp. 1194–95.

99. Ibid., p. 572.

100. Hidy and Hidy, *Pioneering in Big Business*, pp. 112, 118.

101. Martin, *James J. Hill*, pp. 228, 407.

102. Harold U. Faulkner, *The Decline of Laissez Faire* (New York: Rinehart, 1951), pp. 166–67.

103. Grodinsky, *Jay Gould*, p. 115, citing *Transportation interests of the United States and Canada*, report no. 847, Senate, 51st Cong. 1st sess., 1890, p. 150.

104. John Murray Forbes, president, C.B.&Q., to N. W. Beckwith, unidentified, March 30, 1881, cited in Cochran, *Railroad Leaders*, p. 339.

105. U.S., Industrial Commission, 4:144; 9:491.

106. Ibid., 4:343; 9:88, 291, 373.

107. Ibid., 4:501; 9:486; 13:107-08.

108. Ibid., 19:405, 409-10, 414-15, 618.

109. Marian V. Sears, "The American Businessman at the Turn of the Century," *Business History Review* 30 (December 1956): 442-43.

110. U. S., Industrial Commission, 1:111, 118; 13:467, 473, 497.

111. Ibid., 1:13-14, pt. I.

112. U.S., Senate *Report of the Senate upon the Relations between Labor and Capital*, 48th Cong., 2d sess. (Washington, D.C.: Government Printing Office, 1885) 1:1074.

113. Martin, *James J. Hill*, pp. 413-14.

114. Evelyn H. Knowlton, *Pepperell's Progress* (Cambridge, Mass.: Harvard University Press, 1948), p. 224; Williamson, *Winchester*, pp. 132-33.

115. Stuart Daggett, *Railroad Reorganization* (Boston: Houghton Mifflin, 1908), pp. 21-22.

116. Edward Mott, *Between the Ocean and the Lakes* (New York: John S. Collins, 1899), pp. 277-78.

117. Grodinsky, *Jay Gould*, pp. 358-59, 414.

118. Daggett, *Railroad Reorganization*, p. 208.

119. L. L. Waters, *Steel Trails to Santa Fe* (Lawrence, Kan.: University of Kansas Press, 1950), p. 210.

120. Charles Elliott Perkins, vice-president, C.B.&Q., to John Murray Forbes, president, March 10, 1881, cited in Cochran, *Railroad Leaders*, p. 185.

121. Charles Elliott Perkins, president, C.B.&Q., to Thomas J. Potter, vice-president, December 22, 1884, ibid., p. 438.

122. Knowlton, *Pepperell's Progress*, p. 224.

123. Charles Elliott Perkins, president, C.B.&Q., to Thomas J. Potter, vice-president, October 9, 1884, cited in Cochran, *Railroad Leaders*, p. 437.

124. Milton H. Smith to C. C. Baldwin, September 7, 1883, cited in Klein, *Louisville & Nashville Railroad*, p. 188.

125. Cochran, *Railroad Leaders*, p. 89.

126. Stuyvesant Fish, vice-president, Illinois Central, to James C. Clarke, president, January 31, 1886, ibid., p. 318.

127. U.S., Industrial Commission, 9:740.

128. Waters, *Steel Trails*, pp. 195–96, 207, 212; Marshall, *Santa Fe*, p. 246; Daggett, *Railroad Reorganization*, p. 209.

129. Pound and Moore, *More They Told Barron*, pp. 141, 145.

130. U.S., Industrial Commission, 9:457, 466, 740.

131. Cochran, *Railroad Leaders*, p. 226.

132. U.S., Industrial Commission, 1:1032; 4:236, 270, 274.

133. Ibid., 1:1186; 4:286; 9:2.

134. Ibid., 4:286; 297, 313, 658.

135. Ibid., 9:767.

136. Ibid., 1:1195; 4:335.

137. Ibid., 1:102.

138. Sidney Roberts, "Portrait of a Robber Baron: Charles T. Yerkes," *Business History Review* 35 (Autumn 1961): 352, quoting *Chicago* (Evening) *Journal*, January 29, 1898.

139. Ibid., quoting Edwin Le Fevre, "What Availeth It," *Everybody's Magazine*, 24 (June 1911): 839.

140. Lewis Corey, *The House of Morgan* (New York: Watt, 1930), p. 173, quoting *New York Tribune*, December 17, 1890.

141. Taussig, *Ethics of Railway Management*, pp. 4, 5, 6, 20, 76. Taussig began as a physician, became president of what became the St. Louis Terminal Railroad Association from 1869 to 1896, and was also a bank director. He was a political associate of Carl Schurz and similar minded men. For a biographical sketch, see Irving Dilliard, "William Taussig," in *Dictionary of American Biography*, 18:311–12.

142. Thomas Fletcher Oakes, vice-president, Northern Pacific, to R. W. Newport, general land agent, January 7, 1882, cited in Cochran, *Railroad Leaders*, p. 412.

143. Henry Villard, director, Oregon and Caslifornia, to J. W. Dolph, director, January 3, 1882, ibid., p. 482.

CHAPTER 4

1. *Railway Age Gazette*, December 19, 1913, pp. 1197–98.

2. George Kennan, *E. H. Harriman* (Boston: Houghton Mifflin, 1922), 2:42–48.

3. Ibid., p. 48.

4. John F. Stover, *History of the Illinois Central Railroad* (New York: Macmillan, 1975), p. 242.

5. Thomas W. Mitchell, "The Growth of the Union Pacific and Its Financial Operations," *Quarterly Journal of Economics* 21 (August 1907): 610.

6. Donald McConnell, *Economic Virtues in the United States* (New York, 1930), pp. 106, 109.

7. Arthur Pound and Samuel Taylor Moore, eds., *They Told Barron* (New York: Harpers, 1930), p. 86.

8. Ralph W. Hidy and Muriel E. Hidy, *Pioneering in Big Business* (New York: Harpers, 1955) p. 793, n. 13.

9. R. Carlyle Buley, *The Equitable Life Assurance Society of the United States, 1859–1964* (New York: Appleton-Century-Crofts, 1967), 1:572–87.

10. Douglass C. North, "Life Insurance and Investment Banking at the Time of the Armstrong Investigation of 1905–1906," *Journal of Economic History* 14 (Summer 1954): 211, n. 12 citing Armstrong Investigation, pp. 4143–48.

11. R. Carlyle Buley, *The Equitable Life Assurance Society of the United States* (New York: Appleton-Century-Crofts, 1959), p. 102.

12. North, "Life Insurance and Investment Banking," pp. 215, 226.

13. Ibid., p. 226, n. 57; Burton J. Hendrick, *The Story of Life Insurance* (New York: McClure, Phillips & Co., 1907), pp. 223–34.

14. Morton Keller, *The Life Insurance Enterprise, 1885–1910* (Cambridge, Mass.: Harvard University Press, 1963), p. 171.

15. Buley, *Equitable Life Assurance Society of the United States, 1859–1964*, 1:674–75; Keller, *Life Insurance Enterprise*, p. 246.

16. Marquis James, *The Metropolitan Life* (New York: Viking Press, 1947), p. 151.

17. Shepard B. Clough, *A Century of the Mutual Life Insurance Company of New York* (New York: Columbia University Press, 1946), pp. 189–90, 192–93.

18. Merlo J. Pusey, *Charles Evans Hughes* (New York: Macmillan, 1951), 1:160.

19. Louis D. Brandeis, *Other People's Money* (New York: Stokes, 1914), pp. 23, 56, 86.

20. Pusey, *Charles Evans Hughes*, 1:160.

21. John A. Garraty, *Right-Hand Man* (New York: Harpers, 1960), p. 85.

22. Keller, *Life Insurance Enterprise, p. 178.*

23. Ibid., p. 171; Pusey, *Charles Evans Hughes*, 1:158.

24. New York State Legislature, *Testimony Taken before the Joint Committee of the Senate and Assembly of the State of New York to Investigate and Examine into the Business and Affairs of Life Insurance Companies Doing Business in the State of New York* (1905–06), 3:2925, 2930–31 (hereafter cited as *Armstrong Hearings*); Garraty, *Right-Hand Man*, pp. 176–77, 178.

25. Harold F. Williamson and Orange A. Smalley, *Northwestern Mutual Life* (Evanston, Ill.: Northwestern University Press, 1957), pp. 141, 143.

26. U.S. Congress, House Committee on Banking and Currency, Money Trust Investigation, 62d Cong., 3d sess. (Washington, D.C.: Government Printing Office, 1913) 2:1019. Hereafter cited as Money Trust.

27. Ibid., 2:1617.

28. Ibid., 3:156, 1642–43, 1677–78, 1975–76, Report.

29. Ibid., pp. 1982, 2001–02, 2036.

30. Ibid., pp. 157–58, Report.

31. Warren C. Scoville, *Revolution in Glassmaking* (Cambridge, Mass.: Harvard University Press, 1948), pp. 106–08.

32. Thomas C. Cochran, *The Pabst Brewing Company* (New York: New York University Press, 1948), pp. 230–31.

33. Money Trust, 1:6–94; Margaret L. Coit, *Mr. Baruch* (Boston: Houghton Mifflin, 1957), p. 101; Bernard M. Baruch, *My Own Story* (New York: Holt, 1957), pp. 251–53.

34. Brandeis, *Other People's Money*, pp. 44–45.

35. Money Trust, 3:1665.

36. Ibid., pp. 1858–59, 2045.

37. J. P. Morgan and Co., "Letter from Messrs. J. P. Morgan & Company in Response to the Invitation of the Sub-Committee (Hon. A. P. Pujo, Chairman) of the Committee on Banking and Currency of the House of Representatives," (New York, February 25, 1913), p. 19.

38. Money Trust, 1:188, 289, 529.

39. Ibid., pp. 548, 559.

40. Eliot Jones, *The Anthracite Coal Combination in the United States* (Cambridge, Mass.: Harvard University Press, 1914), pp. 59, 132.

41. Jules I. Bogen, *The Anthracite Railroads* (New York: Ronald Press, 1927), p. 215.

42. Jones, *Anthracite Coal Combination*, pp. 74–82, 151, 161, 172.

43. U.S., Industrial Commission, Reports of the Industrial Commission, 19 vols. (Washington, D.C.: Government Printing Office, 1900–02) 9:550.

44. Albro Martin, "The Troubled Subject of Railroad Regulation—A Reappraisal," *Journal of American History* 61 (September 1974): 352, 361–63.

45. David T. Gilchrist, "Albert Fink and the Pooling System," *Business History Review* 34 (Spring 1960): 49.

46. Henry R. Seager and Charles A. Gulick, *Trust and Corporation Problems* (New York: Harpers, 1929), pp. 377, 383.

47. Ibid., p. 385.

48. Edward C. Kirkland, *Industry Comes of Age* (New York: Holt, Rinehart & Winston, 1961), p. 323.

49. Ibid.

50. Scoville, *Revolution in Glassmaking*, pp. 108–09.

51. Alfred D. Chandler, Jr., and Stephen Salsbury, *Pierre S. du Pont and the Making of the Modern Corporation* (New York: Harper & Row, 1971), pp. 81–82, 112, 117, 259–300.

52. Harold F. Williamson, *Winchester* (Washington, D.C.: Combat Forces Press, 1952), pp. 201, 266.

53. Harold F. Williamson and Kenneth H. Myers, *Designed for Digging* (Evanston, Ill.: Northwestern University Press, 1955), p. 96.

54. Eliot Jones, *The Trust Problem in the United States* (New York: Macmillan, 1921), pp. 225–29.

55. Alfred D. Chandler, Jr., *The Visible Hand* (Cambridge, Mass.: Harvard University Press, 1977), pp. 126, 136.

56. William Z. Ripley, *Railroads: Rates and Regulation* (New York: Longmans, Green, 1920), p. 492; Hidy and Hidy, *Pioneering in Big Business*, pp. 456–58; George S. Gibb and Evelyn H. Knowlton, *The Resurgent Years* (New York: Harpers, 1956), pp. 171–72.

57. Ripley, *Railroads*, pp. 207, 215; Allan Nevins, *Study in Power* (New York: Scribner's, 1953), 1:69; Cochran, *Pabst Brewing Company*, p. 181.

58. Ripley, *Railroads*, pp. 209, 213–14.

59. Nevins, *Study in Power*, 2:356–60; Hidy and Hidy, *Pioneering in Big Business*, pp. 676–82.

60. Nevins, *Study in Power*, 2:365–66.

61. Ripley, *Railroads*, p. 214.

62. J. Owen Stalson, *Marketing Life Insurance* (Cambridge, Mass.: Harvard University Press, 1942), pp. 486, 535.

63. Ibid., p. 606; Harris Proschansky, "The National Association of Life Underwriters" (Ph.D. dis., New York University, 1954), p. 259; Buley, *Equitable Life Assurance Society 1859–1964*, 1:552–53.

64. Keller, *Life Insurance Enterprise*, p. 72.

65. Proschansky, "National Association of Life Underwriters," p. 178; Buley, *Equitable Life Assurance Society, 1859–1964*, 1:338, 338n.

66. Williamson and Smalley, *Northwestern Mutual Life*, p. 111 citing Wisconsin Legislature: *Report of the Joint Committee of Senate and Assembly on the Affairs of the Insurance Companies*, 1907, 610; Spencer L. Kimball, *Insurance and Public Policy* (Madison, Wis.: University of Wisconsin Press, 1960), p. 125.

67. Proschansky, "National Association of Life Underwriters," p. 238.

68. Stalson, *Marketing Life Insurance*, p. 551; Buley, *Equitable Life Assurance Society, 1859–1964*, 2:713.

69. Proschansky, "National Association of Life Underwriters," pp. 180, 203; Keller, *Life Insurance Enterprise*, p. 266.

70. Stalson, *Marketing Life Insurance*, pp. 549, 551–53; Keller. *Life Insurance Enterprise*, p. 274.

71. Williamson and Smalley, *Northwestern Mutual Life*, p. 143.

72. Stalson, *Marketing Life Insurance*, p. 606; Proschansky, "National Association of Life Underwriters," p. 259; Keller, *Life Insurance Enterprise*, p. 274.

73. Mark Sullivan, *Our Times* (New York: Scribner's, 1929), 2:511, 511, n. 1.

74. James Harvey Young, *The Toadstool Millionaires* (Princeton, N.J.: Princeton University Press, 1961), pp. 207, 210–11.

75. Ralph M. Hower, *The History of an Advertising Agency* (Cambridge, Mass.: Harvard University Press, 1949), p. 93.

76. Young, *Toadstool Millionaires*, pp. 236–37, 239–40.

77. Boris Emmet and John E. Jeuck, *Catalogues and Counters* (Chicago, Ill.: University of Chicago Press, 1950), pp. 176, 247–50.

78. Ibid., pp. 178, 230, 231, 246.

79. Hidy and Hidy, *Pioneering in Big Business*, pp. 335–36, 468, 692; Chandler and Salsbury, *Pierre S. du Pont*, p. 85.

80. Virginia Huck, *Brand of the Tartan* (New York: Appleton-Century-Crofts, 1955), pp. 43–44.

81. Allan Nevins and Frank E. Hill, *Ford* (New York: Scribner's, 1954), p. 226.

82. Scoville, *Revolution in Glassmaking*, pp. 103–04, p. 104, n. 67.

83. Gibb and Knowlton, *Resurgent Years*, p. 90.

84. Money Trust, 3:1992–93.

85. Gibb and Knowlton, *Resurgent Years*, p. 22.

86. Hidy and Hidy, *Pioneering in Big Business*, p. 468.

87. Chandler, *Visible Hand*, p. 174.

88. Albro Martin, *James J. Hill and the Opening of the Northwest* (New York: Oxford University Press, 1976), p. 537.

89. Gabriel Kolko, *The Triumph of Conservatism* (New York: Free Press, 1963), p. 264.

90. Benjamin Graham and David L. Dodd, *Security Analysis* (New York: McGraw-Hill, 1934), p. 306.

91. Frederick Lewis Allen, *The Lords of Creation* (New York: Harpers, 1935), pp. 48–49.

92. Albro Martin, *Enterprise Denied* (New York: Columbia University Press, 1971), pp. 84–91.

93. James C. Bonbright, *Railroad Capitalization* (New York: Columbia University Press, 1920), pp. 15–16; U.S., Industrial Commission, *Final Report of the Industrial Commission,* (Washington, D.C.: Government Printing Office, 1902), 19:412–15.

94. Vincent P. Carosso, *Investment Banking in America* (Cambridge, Mass.: Harvard University Press, 1970), p. 158; Richard M. Abrams, "Brandeis and the New Haven-Boston & Maine Merger Battle Revisited," *Business History Review* 36 (Winter 1962): 422, 427.

95. William Z. Ripley, *Railroads: Finance and Organization* (New York: Longmans, Green, 1920), pp. 301–03.

96. Kent Healy, *The Economics of Transportation in America* (New York: Ronald Press, 1940), pp. 392–93.

97. Nevins, *Study in Power,* 2:370–71.

98. Seager and Gulick, *Trust and Corporation Problems,* p. 267; Jones, *Trust Problem in the United States,* pp. 236–37; Cyrus McCormick, *Century of the Reaper,* (Boston: Houghton Mifflin, 1931), p. 117; Helen M. Kramer, "Harvesters and High Finance: Formation of the International Harvester Company," *Business History Review* 38 (Autumn 1964): 297.

99. Garraty, *Right-Hand Man,* p. 128; Kramer, "Harvesters and High Finance," p. 292.

100. Garraty, *Right-Hand Man,* p. 131, citing memoranda, June 18, 20, 1902, McCormick Papers.

101. Ibid., p. 136, citing memoranda, July 5, 8, 12, 14, 1902, McCormick Papers.

102. Ibid., p. 137.

103. Graham and Dodd, *Security Analysis,* pp. 306, 308.

104. Benjamin Graham, David L. Dodd, and Sidney Cottle, *Security Analysis* (New York: McGraw-Hill, 1962), p. 213.

105. Arthur S. Dewing, *Corporate Promotions and Reorganizations* (Cambridge, Mass.: Harvard University Press, 1914), p. 12.

106. Theodore F. Marburg, *Small Business in Brass Fabricating* (New York: New York University Press, 1956), p. 48.

107. Carosso, *Investment Banking,* p. 35; Keith L. Bryant, Jr., *History of the Atchison, Topeka and Santa Fe* (New York: Macmillan, 1974), p. 158.

108. Ripley, *Railroads: Rates and Regulation,* pp. 453, 515–16; Healy, *Economics of Transportation,* p. 306.

109. Richard P. Brief, "The Origin and Evolution of Nineteenth-Century Asset Accounting," *Business History Review* 40 (Spring 1966): 17.

110. Chandler, *Visible Hand,* p. 115.

111. David F. Hawkins, "The Development of Modern Financial Re-

porting Practices among American Manufacturing Corporations," *Business History Review* 37 (Autumn 1963): 147, 147, n. 29.

112. C. W. De Mond, *Price, Waterhouse & Co. in America* (New York, 1951), p. 36.

113. Hawkins, "Modern Financial Reporting," p. 140.

114. De Mond, *Price, Waterhouse*, p. 60.

115. Hidy and Hidy, *Pioneering in Big Business*, p. 330.

116. Gibb and Knowlton, *Resurgent Years*, p. 22.

117. Huck, *Brand of the Tartan*, pp. 86–87.

118. Bonbright, *Railroad Capitalization*, pp. 22–23.

119. Pusey, *Charles Evans Hughes*, 1:140–41; Williamson and Smalley, *Northwestern Mutual Life,*, pp. 133–34; Buley, *Equitable Life Assurance Society, 1859–1964*, 1:623–42.

120. Buley, *Equitable Life Assurance Society, 1859–1964*, 2:709.

121. Pusey, *Charles Evans Hughes*, 1:163; James, *Metropolitan Life*, p. 156.

122. Keller, *Life Insurance Enterprise*, p. 183.

123. Pusey, *Charles Evans Hughes*, 1:158, citing Armstrong Hearings, 2:1219; James, *Metropolitan Life*, p. 156, citing Armstrong Hearings, 1:585–88, 594–98, 600–01, 662–64, 706–09; Garraty, *Right-Hand Man*, pp. 171–72, citing Armstrong Hearings, 1:585–88, 600–01; North, "Life Insurance and Investment Banking," p. 225, citing Armstrong Hearings, pp. 348–51, 4736–38.

124. Pusey, *Charles Evans Hughes*, 1:158; James, *Metropolitan Life*, p. 156; Armstrong Hearings 1:587.

125. Frank A. Vanderlip to James Stillman, February 27, 1906, Frank A. Vanderlip Papers, Columbia University.

126. McConnell, *Economic Virtues in the United States*, p. 98.

127. Money Trust, 1:139, 145, 166, 225, 331, 539, 550, 594–95, 653.

128. Pusey, *Charles Evans Hughes*, 1:146; James *Metropolitan Life*, p. 150.

129. Money Trust, 3:1684.

130. Ibid., 1:812; 2:833, 836.

131. Ibid., 2:753. 965.

132. Hidy and Hidy, *Pioneering in Big Business*, pp. 335, 457, 639, 31, 717.

CHAPTER 5

1. Matthew Josephson, *The Robber Barons* (New York: Harcourt, Brace, 1934), p. vii.

2. Richard C. Cabot, *Honesty* (New York: Macmillan, 1938), p. 89.

3. Edmond Cahn, *The Moral Decision* (Bloomington, Ind.: Indiana University Press, 1955), pp. 126–27.

4. Ibid., p. 251.

5. Francis X. Sutton, Seymour E. Harris, Carl Kaysen, and James Tobin, *The American Business Creed* (Cambridge, Mass.: Harvard University Press, 1956), p. 343.

6. Kenneth Wiggins Porter, *The Jacksons and the Lees* (Cambridge, Mass.: Harvard University Press, 1937), 1:100–01, 110.

7. Fritz Redlich, "Sanctions and Freedom of Enterprise," *Journal of Economic History* 11 (Summer 1951): 266–70.

8. J. Owen Stalson, *Marketing Life Insurance* (Cambridge, Mass.: Harvard University Press, 1942), p. 406.

9. David P. Gagan, "The Railroads and the Public, 1870–1881: Charles Elliott Perkins' Business Ethics," *Business History Review* 39 (Spring 1965): 51.

10. Daniel Hodas, *The Business Career of Moses Taylor* (New York: New York University Press, 1976), p. 219.

11. Thomas Turner and Jugh Johnston, "Conscience of a Capitalist: Charles E. Perkins (Paper presented to Business History Conference, Kent State University, 1965), pp. 78–80; Albro Martin, *James J. Hill and the Opening of the Northwest* (New York: Oxford University Press, 1976), pp. 431, 469–70.

12. Maury Klein, *History of the Louisville & Nashville Railroad* (New York: Macmillan, 1972), p. 203.

13. Gagan, "The Railroads and the Public," p. 43.

14. Thomas C. Cochran, "Role and Sanction in American Entrepreneurial History," in *Change and the Entrepreneur* (Cambridge, Mass.: Harvard University Press, 1949), p. 166.

15. Stalson, *Marketing Life Insurance*, p. 295.

16. Irwin G. Wyllie, *The Self-Made Man in America* (New Brunswick, N.J.: Rutgers University Press, 1954), p. 76.

17. Mark Sullivan, *Our Times* (New York: Scribner's, 1929), 2:521, n. 1.

18. Klein, *Louisville & Nashville Railroad*, pp. 199–200.

19. Thomas C. Cochran, "The Entrepreneur in Economic Change," *Explorations in Entrepreneurial History/Second Series* 3 (Fall 1965): 36–37.

20. Stalson, *Marketing Life Insurance*, pp. 294–95.

21. Robert H. Wiebe, *Businessmen and Reform* (Cambridge, Mass.: Harvard University Press, 1962), p. 218, quoting *Annual Statement of the Memphis Merchants' Exchange, 1904*, pp. 15–19.

22. Redlich, "Sanctions and Freedom of Enterprise," pp. 266–70.

23. Stuart Daggett, *Chapters on the History of the Southern Pacific* (New York: Ronald Press, 1922), p. 239.

24. Ralph W. Hidy and Muriel E. Hidy, *Pioneering in Big Business* (New York: Harpers, 1955), p. 716.

25. Cochran, "Role and Sanction in American Entrepreneurial History," p. 175.

26. Edwin H. Sutherland, "Is 'White Collar Crime' Crime?" *American Sociological Review* 10 (April 1955): 138; Marshall B. Clinard, *The Black Market* (New York: Rinehart, 1952), 230.

27. Edwin H. Sutherland, *White Collar Crime* (New York: Dryden, 1949), pp. 219, 222; Clinard, *The Black Market*, p. 306.

BIBLIOGRAPHY

Abrams, Richard M. "Brandeis and the New Haven-Boston & Maine Merger Battle Revisited." *Business History Review* 36 (Winter 1962): 408–30.

Adams, Charles Francis, Jr., and Henry Adams. *Chapters of Erie.* New York: Holt, 1886.

Allen, Frederick Lewis. *The Lords of Creation.* New York: Harpers, 1935.

Baruch, Bernard M. *My Own Story* New York: Holt, 1957.

Benson, Lee. *Merchants, Farmers, & Railroads.* Cambridge, Mass.: Harvard University Press, 1955.

Bogen, Jules I. *The Anthracite Railroads.* New York: Ronald Press, 1927.

Bok, Edward. *The Americanization of Edward Bok.* New York: Scribner's, 1924.

Bonbright, James C. *Railroad Capitalization.* New York: Columbia University Press, 1920.

Brandeis, Louis D. *Other People's Money.* New York: Stokes, 1914.

Bridge, James Howard. *The Inside Story of the Carnegie Steel Company.* New York: Aldine, 1903.

Brief, Richard P. "The Origin and Evolution of Nineteenth-Century Asset Accounting." *Business History Review* 40 (Spring 1966): 1–23.

Bryant, Keith L., Jr. *History of the Atchison, Topeka and Santa Fe.* New York: Macmillan, 1974.

Buley, R. Carlyle. *The Equitable Life Assurance Society of the United States.* New York: Appleton-Century-Crofts, 1959.

———. *The Equitable Life Assurance Society of the United States, 1859–1964.* New York: Appleton-Century-Crofts, 1967.

Cabot, Richard C. *Honesty.* New York: Macmillan, 1938.

Cahn, Edmond. *The Moral Decision.* Bloomington, Ind.: Indiana University Press, 1955.

Carosso, Vincent P. *Investment Banking in America*. Cambridge, Mass.: Harvard University Press, 1970.

Chandler, Alfred D., Jr. *Henry Varnum Poor*. Cambridge, Mass.: Harvard University Press, 1956.

———.*The Visible Hand*. Cambridge, Mass.: Harvard University Press, 1977.

Chandler, Alfred D., Jr., and Salsbury, Stephen. *Pierre S. du Pont and the Making of the Modern Corporation*. New York: Harper & Row, 1971.

Clark, John Maurice. *The Ethical Basis of Human Freedom*. New York: Kazanjian Foundation Lectures, 1955.

Clinard, Marshall B. *The Black Market*. New York: Rinehart, 1952.

Clough, Shepard B. *A Century of the Mutual Life Insurance Company of New York*. New York: Columbia University Press, 1946.

Cochran, Thomas C. "The Entrepreneur in Economic Change," *Explorations in Entrepreneurial History/Second Series* 3 (Fall 1965): 25–37.

———. "Henry Villard: Entrepreneur." In Edward N. Saveth, ed., *Understanding the American Past*, pp. 352–67. Boston: Little, Brown, 1954.

———. *The Pabst Brewing Company*. New York: New York University Press, 1948.

———. *Railroad Leaders, 1845–1890*. Cambridge, Mass.: Harvard University Press, 1953.

———. "Role and Sanction in American Entrepreneurial History." In *Change and the Entrepreneur*, pp. 153–75. Cambridge, Mass.: Harvard University Press, 1949.

Cochran, Thomas C., and Miller, William. *The Age of Enterprise*. New York: Macmillan, 1942.

Coit, Margaret L. *Mr. Baruch*. Boston: Houghton Mifflin, 1957.

Cole, Arthur H. *Business Enterprise in Its Social Setting*. Cambridge: Harvard University Press, 1959.

Coolidge, T. Jefferson. *Autobiography*. Boston: Houghton Mifflin, 1923.

Corey, Lewis. *The House of Morgan*. New York: Watt, 1930.

Daggett, Stuart. *Chapters on the History of the Southern Pacific*. New York: Ronald Press, 1922.

———. *Railroad Reorganization*.Boston: Houghton Mifflin, 1908.

Davis, John P. *The Union Pacific Railway*. Chicago: S. G. Griggs, 1894.

DeMond, C. W. *Price, Waterhouse & Co. in America*. New York, 1951.

Destler, Chester McArthur. "The Standard Oil, Child of the Erie Ring, 1868–1872." *Mississippi Valley Historical Review* 33 (June 1946): 89–114.

Dewing, Arthur S. *Corporate Promotions and Reorganizations*. Cambridge, Mass.: Harvard University Press, 1914.

Emmet, Boris, and Jeuck, John. *Catalogues and Counters.* Chicago: University of Chicago Press, 1950.

Ewing, John S., and Norton, Nancy P. *Broadlooms and Businessmen.* Cambridge: Harvard University Press, 1955.

Faulkner, Harold U. *The Decline of Laissez Faire.* New York: Rinehart, 1951.

Gagan, David P. "The Railroads and the Public, 1870-1881: Charles Elliott Perkins' Business Ethics." *Business History Review* 39 (Spring 1965): 41-65.

Garraty, John A. *Right-Hand Man.* New York: Harpers, 1960.

Gates, Paul Wallace. *The Illinois Central Railroad and Its Colonization Work.* Cambridge, Mass.: Harvard University Press, 1934.

Gibb, George S. and Knowlton, Evelyn H. *The Resurgent Years.* New York: Harpers, 1956.

Gilchrist, David T. "Albert Fink and the Pooling System." *Business History Review* 34 (Spring 1960): 24-49.

Graham, Benjamin, and Dodd, David L. *Security Analysis.* New York: McGraw-Hill, 1934.

Graham, Benjamin; Dodd, David L.; and Cottle, Sidney. *Security Analysis.* New York: McGraw-Hill, 1962.

Grodinsky, Julius. *Jay Gould.* Philadelphia: University of Pennsylvania Press, 1957.

Hadley, Arthur Twining. *Standards of Public Morality.* New York: Macmillan, 1907.

Harlow, Alvin F. *The Road of the Century.* New York: Creative Age Press, 1947.

Harvey, George. *Henry Clay Frick.* New York: Scribner's, 1928.

Hawkins, David F. "The Development of Modern Financial Reporting Practices among American Manufacturing Corporations." *Business History Review* 37 (Autumn 1963): 135-68.

Healy, Kent. *The Economics of Transportation in America.* New York: Ronald Press, 1940.

Hendrick, Burton J. *The Story of Life Insurance.* New York: McClure, Phillips & Co., 1907.

Hidy, Ralph W., and Hidy, Muriel E. *Pioneering in Big Business.* New York: Harpers, 1955.

Hodas, Daniel. *The Business Career of Moses Taylor.* New York: New York University Press, 1976.

Hower, Ralph M. *The History of an Advertising Agency.* Cambridge, Mass.: Harvard University Press, 1949.

Huck, Virginia. *Brand of the Tartan.* New York; Appleton-Century-Crofts, 1955.

Hughes, Sarah Forbes, ed. *Letters and Recollections of John Murray Forbes*. Boston: Houghton Mifflin, 1900.

Hungerford, Edward. *Men and Iron*. New York: Crowell, 1938.

———. *Men of Erie*. New York: Random House, 1946.

Hunter, Louis C. *Steamboats on the Western Rivers*. Cambridge, Mass.: Harvard University Press, 1949.

———. *Studies in the Economic History of the Ohio Valley*. Smith College Studies in History, Volume 19. Northampton, Mass.: Smith College, 1933–1934.

Huxley, Aldous. *Ends and Means*. New York: Harpers, 1937.

James, Marquis. *The Metropolitan Life*. New York: Viking Press, 1947.

Jones, Eliot. *The Anthracite Coal Combination in the United States*. Cambridge, Mass.: Harvard University Press, 1914.

———. *The Trust Problem in the United States*. New York: Macmillan, 1921.

Josephson, Matthew. *The Robber Barons*. New York: Harcourt, Brace, 1934.

Keller, Morton. *The Life Insurance Enterprise, 1885–1910*. Cambridge, Mass.: Harvard University Press, 1963.

Kennan, George. *E. H. Harriman*. Boston: Houghton Mifflin, 1922.

Kimball, Spencer L. *Insurance and Public Policy*. Madison: University of Wisconsin Press, 1960.

Kirkland, Edward Chase. *Charles Francis Adams, Jr., 1835–1915*. Cambridge, Mass.: Harvard University Press, 1965.

———. *Industry Comes of Age*. New York: Holt, Rinehart & Winston, 1961.

———. *Men, Cities and Transportation*. Cambridge, Mass.: Harvard University Press, 1948.

Klein, Maury. *History of the Louisville & Nashville Railroad*. New York: Macmillan, 1972.

Knowlton, Evelyn H. *Pepperell's Progress*. Cambridge, Mass.: Harvard University Press, 1948.

Kolko, Gabriel. *The Triumph of Conservatism* New York: Free Press, 1963.

Kramer, Helen M. "Harvesters and High Finance: Formation of the International Harvester Company." *Business History Review* 38 (Autumn 1964): 283–301.

Lane, Wheaton H. *Commodore Vanderbilt*. New York: Knopf, 1942.

McConnell, Donald. *Economic Virtues in the United States*. New York, 1930.

McCormick, Cyrus. *Century of the Reaper*. Boston: Houghton Mifflin, 1931.

Marburg, Theodore F. *Small Business in Brass Fabricating*. New York: New York University Press, 1956.

Marshall, James. *Santa Fe*. New York: Random House, 1945.

Martin, Albro. *Enterprise Denied*. New York: Columbia University Press, 1971.

———. *James J. Hill and the Opening of the Northwest*. New York: Oxford University Press, 1976.

———. "The Troubled Subject of Railroad Regulation— A Reappraisal." *Journal of American History* 61 (September 1974): 339-71.

Meyer, Balthasar Henry, ed. *History of Transportation in the United States before 1860*. Washington, D.C.: Carnegie Institution, 1917.

Mitchell, Thomas W. "The Growth of the Union Pacific and Its Financial Operations." *Quarterly Journal of Economics* 21 (August 1907): 569-612.

Morison, Samuel Eliot. *The Ropemakers of Plymouth*. Boston: Houghton Mifflin, 1950.

Mott, Edward. *Between the Ocean and the Lakes*. New York: John S. Collins, 1899.

Neu, Irene D. *Erastus Corning*. Ithaca, N.Y.: Cornell University Press, 1960.

Nevins, Allan. *Abram S. Hewitt*. New York: Harpers, 1935.

———. *Study in Power*. New York: Scribner's, 1953.

———, and Hill, Frank E. *Ford*. New York: Scribner's, 1954.

New York State Legislature. *Testimony Taken before the Joint Committee of the Senate and Assembly of the State of New York to Investigate and Examine into the Business and Affairs of Life Insurance Companies Doing Business in the State of New York*. Albany, N.Y., 1905-1906.

———. Assembly. *Proceedings of the Special Committee on Railroads, Appointed under a Resolution of the Assembly, February 28, 1879, to Investigate Alleged Abuses in the Management of Railroads Chartered by the State of New York, A. B. Hepburn, Chairman*. New York, 1879.

North, Douglass C. "Life Insurance and Investment Banking at the Time of the Armstrong Investigation of 1905-1906." *Journal of Economic History* 14 (Summer 1954): 209-28.

Overton, Richard C. *Burlington Route*. New York: Knopf, 1965.

———. *Gulf to Rockies*. Austin: University of Texas Press, 1953.

Passer, Harold. *The Electrical Manufacturers*. Cambridge, Mass.: Harvard University Press, 1953.

Pearson, Henry Greenleaf. *An American Railroad Builder*. Boston: Houghton Mifflin, 1911.

Pierce, Harry H. *Railroads of New York*. Cambridge, Mass.: Harvard University Press, 1953.

Porter, Kenneth Wiggins. *The Jacksons and the Lees.* Cambridge, Mass.: Harvard University Press, 1937.

Pound, Arthur, and Moore, Samuel Taylor, eds. *More They Told Barron.* New York: Harpers, 1931.

———. *They Told Barron.* New York: Harpers, 1930.

Presbrey, Frank. *The History and Development of Advertising.* Garden City, N.Y.: Doubleday, Doran, 1929.

Proschansky, Harris. "The National Association of Life Underwriters." Ph. D. dissertation, New York University, 1954.

Pusey, Merlo J. *Charles Evans Hughes.* New York: Macmillan, 1951.

Redlich, Fritz. "Sanctions and Freedom of Enterprise." *Journal of Economic History* 11 (Summer 1951): 266–72.

Ripley, William Z. *Railroads: Finance and Organization.* New York: Longmans, Green, 1920.

———. *Railroads: Rates and Regulation.* New York: Longmans, Green, 1920.

Roberts, Sidney. "Portrait of a Robber Baron: Charles T. Yerkes." *Business History Review* 35 (Autumn 1961): 344–71.

Schlesinger, Arthur M., Jr. *The Age of Jackson.* Boston: Little, Brown, 1946.

Schumpeter, Joseph A. *Business Cycles.* New York: McGraw-Hill, 1939.

Scoville, Warren C. *Revolution in Glassmaking.* Cambridge, Mass.: Harvard University Press, 1948.

Seager, Henry R., and Gulick, Charles A. *Trust and Corporation Problems.* New York: Harpers, 1929.

Sears, Marian V. "The American Businessman at the Turn of the Century." *Business History Review* 30 (December 1956): 382–443.

Sharp, Frank Chapman, and Fox, Philip F. *Business Ethics.* New York: Appleton-Century, 1937.

Stalson, J. Owen. *Marketing Life Insurance.* Cambridge, Mass.: Harvard University Press, 1942.

Stevens, Frank Walker. *The Beginnings of the New York Central Railroad.* New York: Putnam, 1926.

Stover, John F. *History of the Illinois Central Railroad.* New York: Macmillan, 1975.

Sullivan, Mark. *Our Times.* New York: Scribner's 1929.

Sutherland, Edwin H. "Is 'White Collar Crime' Crime?" *American Sociological Review* 10 (April 1955): 132–39.

———. *White Collar Crime.* New York: Dryden, 1949.

Sutton, Francis X.; Harris, Seymour E.; Kaysen, Carl; and Tobin, James. *The American Business Creed.* Cambridge, Mass.: Harvard University Press, 1956.

Taussig, William. *Ethics of Railway Management.* St. Louis, Mo.: R. P. Studley, 1898.

Taylor, George Rogers. *The Transportation Revolution.* New York: Rinehart, 1951.

Turner, Thomas, and Johnston, Hugh. "Conscience of a Capitalist: Charles E. Perkins," presented at Business History Conference, Kent State University, 1965.

U.S., Congress, House Committee on Currency and Banking, Money Trust (Pujo) Investigation, *Investigation of Financial and Monetary Conditions in the United States, 62d Cong., 2d sess.,* Washington, D.C.: Government Printing Office, 1913.

U.S., Congress, Senate Committee on Education and Labor, *Report of the Senate upon the Relations between Labor and Capital,* 48th Cong., 2d sess., Washington D.C.: Government Printing Office, 1885.

U.S., Industrial Commission, *Reports of the Industrial Commission,* Washington, D.C.: Government Printing Office, 1900.

Wall, Joseph Frazier. *Andrew Carnegie.* New York: Oxford University Press, 1970.

Waters, L. L. *Steel Trails to Santa Fe.* Lawrence, Kan.: University of Kansas Press, 1950.

Wiebe, Robert H. *Businessmen and Reform.* Cambridge, Mass.: Harvard University Press, 1962.

Williamson, Harold F. *Edward Atkinson.* Boston: Old Corner Book Store, 1934.

———. *Winchester.* Washington, D.C.: Combat Forces Press, 1952.

Williamson, Harold F., and Daum, Arnold R. *The Age of Illumination.* Evanston, Ill.: Northwestern University Press, 1959.

Williamson, Harold F., and Myers, Kenneth H. *Designed for Digging.* Evanston, Ill.: Northwestern University Press, 1955.

Williamson, Harold F., and Smalley, Orange A. *Northwestern Mutual Life.* Evanston, Ill.: Northwestern University Press, 1957.

Wyllie, Irwin G. *The Self-Made Man in America.* New Brunswick, N.J.: Rutgers University Press, 1954.

Young, James Harvey. *The Toadstool Millionaires.* Princeton: Princeton University Press, 1961.

INDEX

ABOUT THE AUTHOR

Saul Engelbourg is Associate Professor of History at Boston University.
He is the author of articles for *Business History, Business History Review,*
and other journals.